OFFICE
INFLUENCE

GET WHAT YOU WANT,
FROM THE MAILROOM TO THE BOARDROOM

ERIC P. BLOOM

AVIVA
PUBLISHING
New York

TO MARTHA,
THANK YOU FOR
YOUR HELP AND
SUPPORT. IT'S A
PLEASURE WORKING
WITH YOU!

Eric

Office Influence:
Get What You Want, From the Mailroom to the Boardroom

Published by:
Aviva Publishing
Lake Placid, NY, USA
(515) 523-1320
www.AvivaPubs.com

Eric Bloom
eric.bloom@ITMLinstitute.org
www.OfficeInfluence.com

ISBN: 978-1-947937-87-1

Library of Congress Control Number: 2019902108
Editors: Lee Berman, and Larry Alexander and Tyler Tichelaar, Superior Book Productions
Cover Designer: Meredith Lindsay
Interior Book Designer: Meredith Lindsay
Author Photo: Rich Powers

Every attempt has been made to source properly all quotes.
Printed in the United States of America

To Micah and Jolie,
So young, but so loved.
Welcome to the world!

Love, Grandpa

ACKNOWLEDGMENTS

A book of this type is not just written solely out of the mind of the author. The insights within it have fermented over the years and come from a variety of sources, both business and personal, including:

- My students who asked great questions, forcing me to dig deeply for (hopefully) insightful answers, which in turn caused me to look at influence in new ways.

- Those I've worked with—my managers, peers, and staff—who have tried to influence me to my or their benefit or detriment, and whom I realized—long after the fact—changed my actions.

- Politicians of all parties who are well schooled in influence and body language whom I've observed on TV or in-person.

- The giants of influence thought leadership who sparked my interest in the study of influence, some of whom are mentioned in this book. Their contributions to the field of influence are truly immeasurable.

- My children when they were young, trying to stay up an extra hour on a school night or have a cookie before dinner.

- My fellow speakers in the National Speakers Association, who are among the most brilliant, motivated, and articulate people I have ever had the honor to call my friends.

In addition to those previously mentioned, this book has taken a village to create.

My wife Cheryl has been a great sounding board, inspiration, and willing partner in working through various concepts and topics. She also exhibited the patience of Job with her willingness to listen while I talked about this book *ad nauseam* throughout the writing process.

I would also like to thank Lee Berman for doing the initial edit on my manuscript, chapter by chapter, typo by typo, and missing word by missing word. Truth be told, I'm moderately dyslexic and have great difficulty proofreading my written words. Lee took the brunt of it when reviewing my work.

As you will see, Part 2 of the book centers around a mathematical formula I call the Influence Power Rating (IPR), which calculates your level of influence within the workplace. The first part of the formula, the Core Influence Characteristics, contains seventy-four personal and business attributes that can positively or negatively affect your ability to influence others. The research behind the relative effect of each of these attributes was done via a survey created with the assistance of Josh Packard and Megan Bissell at the University of Northern Colorado Media Lab. Their suggestions and assistance were invaluable in the definition and collection of my research data. I would also like to thank the many professional organizations that assisted in my research by providing their membership with the link to my survey. At the time of this writing, these organizations include:

- Business Relationship Management Institute (BRM Institute)
- New England Human Resources Association (NEHRA)
- Society for Information Management (SIM) New Jersey Chapter
- International Institute of Business Analysts (IIBA) Boston Chapter
- Heller Associates
- Association of Talent Management (ATD) Central Mass
- Society for Human Resource Professionals (SHRP) Boston
- New England Electronic Commerce Users' Group (NEECOM)

Lastly, finishing a book's text is only the first step in the publishing process. Bringing it to print also requires the help, guidance, and creativity of a team of publishing-related professionals. I would like to thank Susan Friedmann, Founder of AVIVA Publishing, for her willingness to accept my book for publication, Meredith Lindsay, the creatively brilliant designer of the book's cover and interior design, and Tyler Tichelaar and Larry Alexander for their incredible work proofreading my text.

TABLE OF CONTENTS

INTRODUCTION
YOU SHOULD NOT READ

Every interpersonal endeavor includes an aspect of influence. In negotiation, you're influencing someone to move closer to your point of view. In change management, you're influencing someone to do something differently. In conflict resolution, you're influencing people or organizations to resolve their issues and get along. The list goes on and on.

Certainly, each of these interpersonal communication activities has its own goals, techniques, concepts, and methodologies, but at their core, they all use influence as a tool to achieve an acceptable and defined outcome. That is why it is so important to study influence. When you learn how to influence, you enhance your ability to succeed in all interpersonal interactions.

I'll expand on this theme later in the book, but for now, here are a few examples of how infusing influence techniques into your other activities can enhance your interpersonal communication success.

EXAMPLE #1: NEGOTIATION

Reciprocity is a topic that will be discussed in Chapter 9 on Cialdini's Six Principles of Persuasion. It means that when you do something good for someone, that person will feel a social obligation to do something good for you.

You can use this concept to your advantage by doing small, nice things for those with whom you will be negotiating, before the negotiation begins. For example, if you receive an unsolicited email on a topic you believe may be of interest to the person you will be negotiating with, forward it to the person, simply saying, "I saw this and thought of you." This small action will build goodwill toward you as well as instill in the person a small feeling of obligation to return the favor later, hopefully for you, during the negotiation process.

EXAMPLE #2: CHANGE MANAGEMENT

When implementing change within your company, identify an informal leader within the group being targeted for change. When appropriate, ask for the leader's advice or opinion regarding how the change should be implemented. Then, by using some, or all of their advice and attributing the credit to them, you give them a feeling of ownership toward the project. This will enhance their level of commitment to the change and encourage them to use their informal leadership position to help implement it. As the expression goes, if someone is not part of the solution, they often become part of the problem.

EXAMPLE #3: GAINING AN ADVANTAGE OVER YOUR PEERS

One of the most reliable ways to gain influence over your peers is to be tightly aligned and close friends with your manager. If your peers feel your manager is more likely to take your side than theirs, it gives you unstated delegated authority over those also reporting to your manager.

EXAMPLE #4: RESOLVING A CONFLICT BETWEEN TWO OF YOUR DIRECT REPORTS

Tell your two reports that they will both be in trouble if they don't find a way to work together. You being the bad guy gives them both an excuse to work together without either one of them having to "give in." They can simply agree to disagree and work together to save them both from getting in trouble. As the saying goes, the enemy of my enemy is my friend. By you being their shared conceptual "enemy," you're forming a team and shared goal between them.

The title of this introduction is another example of influential technique. In this case, I've used "Reverse Influence," often called "Reverse Psychology," a trick that parents often joke about using on their children. Namely, if you want your child to do something they don't want to do, tell them not to do it. I won't pass judgment on whether this tactic should or should not be used in child rearing; I'm simply saying it exists. Now back to the adult world; do you always read a book's introduction, or did you read this one because I told you not to? As a second question, how many of your fellow readers do you think followed my instructions and did not read this introduction because I told them not to?

This book is divided into three sections:

Part 1: Key Influence Concepts discusses a variety of important influence-related concepts, definitions, techniques, tactics, and tips.

Part 2: Your Influence Power Rating (IPR) brings together two key influence-related concepts. The first concept helps you identify and build your ability to impress, interact, and gain the respect of others. The second concept is designed to provide an understanding of your ability to influence a predefined person or group on a specific topic at a specific moment.

Part 3: Using Influence provides specific instruction on how the various influence concepts, techniques, tips, and tricks discussed in Parts 1 and 2 can be used to enhance your success in other workplace-related interpersonal activities.

Using techniques like these, to gain influence over those in the workplace, can be done strategically over time or tactically in the moment. It can be done for the good of a person, company, or the world. These techniques can be used to forward an objective that's important to you, or unfortunately, they can also be used to manipulate others to their detriment and your personal gain. Like all scientific discoveries, technological advances, and newly created psychological techniques, the outcome produced depends on the person using it. This is the power of influence. My hope is that you use this power for good, not evil.

[PART 1]

KEY INFLUENCE CONCEPTS

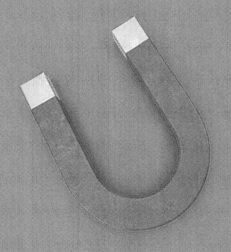

KEY INFLUENCE CONCEPTS

Part 1 of this book discusses a variety of important influence-related concepts, definitions, techniques, tactics, and tips. The goal is to provide you with a solid foundation in the study of influence. It contains a combination of general influence-related knowledge, including well-known research from giants in the study of influence, including Robert B. Cialdini, Allan R. Cohen, and David L. Bradford. It also includes insights from my research and observations.

This combined body of knowledge, while of great value and usability in its own right, is also designed to be a precursor for the book's Parts 2 and 3. Part 2 introduces the Influence Power Rating (IPR) calculation and its key components: Core Influence Characteristics, Situational Knowledge, and Situational Audience. It also describes the seventy-four individual characteristics contained within the calculation. Part 3 provides insights and detailed advice about the influence-based topics learned in Part 1 and can be used to enhance your success in other interpersonal endeavors, including negotiation, organizational change, and others.

The key influence concepts included in Part 1 are:

Return on Investment of Studying Influence: The reason you should spend your time learning and using influence-based techniques in the workplace.

Importance of Personal Connection: All interpersonal activities are enhanced by the same mechanism, a trusted relationship with the individual(s) with whom you are interacting.

Barriers to Influence: Understanding the issues, obstacles, and challenges that can arise when trying to influence others is the first step toward overcoming them.

Seven Key Influence Strategies: When people think about influencing others, they often think about short-term tactics that are sales-like in approach and appearance. While influence techniques can certainly be used this way and for this purpose, other strategies can also be employed.

Push/Pull Influence: Push and pull influence are two sides of the same coin. Push influencers urge or force a person or group to perform a task. Pull influencers attempt to motivate a person or group to want to comply or perform the task at hand.

Influential Types of Communication: There are different techniques you can use, in a seemingly ordinary conversation, that dramatically enhance your ability to influence others. The beauty of these techniques is they are easily incorporated into other types of interpersonal interaction, such as negotiation, conflict resolution, and delegation.

Levels of Commitment: The ability to influence your coworkers is, of course, a very important skill. To maximize its effectiveness, however, you must also know whom to influence.

Cialdini's Six Types of Influence: Robert Cialdini, a thought leader and bestselling author on influence, describes six types of persuasion: reciprocity, commitment/consistency, social proof (safety in numbers), liking, authority, and scarcity.

Cohen-Bradford's Influence Currencies: Allan Cohen and David Bradford, thought leaders and best-selling authors on influence, state "Influence is possible when you have what others want." They describe five types of currency: inspiration-related, task-related, position-related, relationship-related, and personal-related.

Action/Reaction Influencers: These subtle types of influence allow you to gently influence others' actions, simply by how you act toward them.

Building Your Professional Brand: The stronger your professional brand, the greater your influence. This is because people are more willing to take advice, suggestions, and directions from those they respect and admire.

THE RETURN ON INVESTMENT (ROI) OF STUDYING INFLUENCE

The true price of low personal productivity is the cost of lost opportunity.

~Eric Bloom

When I teach my class "Leading through Influence," I always begin with the same exercise, shown in Figure 1. Its purpose is to help my students understand how much time they spend each day trying to influence people to complete the tasks they have already been asked to perform. You can do this for yourself using the worksheet at the end of this chapter.

How much of your work time do you spend influencing others?

Activity	% of Day

Figure 1.1

When the class completes this exercise, the time spent on influence-related activities is noted to be generally between 20 and 75 percent, depending upon job type. Sales professionals, project managers, relationship managers, administrative staff, and managers/executives of all types tend to be in the 50 to 75 percent range. On the lowest end at 5 to 25 percent are people in heads-down, transaction-oriented jobs, such as programmers, accounting staff, and those in operational or process type roles. The general correlation is: the more the role requires dealing with people, the higher the percentage of each day that person will spend trying to influence others.

Your Task

Complete the exercise described in Figure 1.1 using your actual work activities and amount of time spent working to influence others.

This will help you calculate your potential productivity ROI of studying and using influence.

ROI #1: PERSONAL PRODUCTIVITY

For the sake of argument, let's say that 25 percent of your day is spent trying to influence other people to do the tasks they've been assigned. If learning about influence could cut that time in half to 12.5 percent of your day, then based on an eight-hour day, you would save one hour a day, providing you use that time to do other things. Yes, that's five hours per week of reclaimed productivity. This time could be used to perform other important tasks or simply leave the office in time to watch your child's after-school soccer game.

ROI #2: ENHANCED WORK QUALITY

Another advantage of studying influence is it makes it easier to get what you need to perform your job. This could be allocation of money/budget, getting the best people to work on your project, receiving favorable terms from a vendor, or having access to important information. Collectively, these items and others like them allow you to increase the quality of your projects, and they provide you with the opportunity to create your highest quality work.

ROI #3: REDUCED PROJECT/TASK RISK

Continuing on the theme described in ROI #2, if your project is well funded and has the best possible people, information, and vendor support, these factors increase the chances of success by reducing the overall risk.

This reduced risk is advantageous to your company, your department, and, ultimately, you personally.

ROI #4: ENHANCED JOB PERFORMANCE

If you are more productive (ROI #1), your work quality is higher (ROI #2), and your projects/tasks are more likely to succeed (ROI #3), then, logic would dictate, the influence you wield has a positive effect on your overall job performance.

ROI #5: POSITIONS YOU FOR FUTURE PROMOTION OPPORTUNITIES

In addition to the value to the company of the previously stated ROIs, your ability to influence others also helps position you for future career advancement. This is achieved by the combination of:

- Illustrating your ability to lead your peers and others toward a desired objective.

- Showing your ability to get things done.

- Generating great business results.

Percentage of Your Spent Day Influencing Others Worksheet

Your Activites	% of Day Influencing Others on This Activity
Total percent of your day influencing others (add percentage of numbers entered in column 2)	

IMPORTANCE OF PERSONAL CONNECTION

All interpersonal activities are enhanced by the same mechanism, a trusted relationship with the person with whom you are interacting.

~Eric Bloom

I have spent many years designing and teaching classes on various types of interpersonal communication, including: negotiation, change management, conflict, leadership, difficult conversations, motivation, requesting approval, delegation, and others.

All of these interpersonal activities are enhanced by the same mechanism—trusting relationships with the individuals with whom you are interacting. You don't have to be friends. Even though being friends may help, it is not required. Think about your personal experiences. Are you more easily influenced by someone you trust? Are you more likely to go home with a negotiated agreement if you believe the other party will hold up their end of the deal? As a manager, it is more comfortable and less stressful to delegate to someone you know will do their best to complete the task without attempting to undermine you in the process.

This brings us to an interesting question: "How can we build trust in someone we are attempting to influence?"

There are actually two answers to this question. The obvious one is what we were taught as children: Keep your promises. Have a win-win mentality. Be honest. These maxims remain true and should always be followed, but often they are just not enough.

This brings us to the second answer to this question: Strategically, get to know now those you will try to influence in the future through negotiation, change management, or conflict resolution. Although this is not always possible, try. For example: If you are a human resources manager in a new role, reach out to the line managers and executives you are supporting to introduce yourself. Establish rapport with them before you begin to push them to complete their employee performance reviews on time. If you are a salesperson in a new territory, opportunistically "swing by" to meet face-to-face with your customers before you try to make that future sale. If you are a project manager with a team in another country, schedule a Skype call with them to establish a virtual face-to-face relationship before you need to push them to complete an important task by a specific date.

These types of interactions help you establish trust, a professional relationship, and possibly, friendships. The simple act of getting to know someone first dramatically increases the probability that they will follow, help, or support you when the time comes. Certainly, remain professional, but get personal. Find common ground. If you both play tennis, talk tennis. If you both went to the same college or worked at the same company, talk about your common experiences.

If this person is very important to you, such as a major client or a big donor to your charity, do a little research. Search social media—look them up on LinkedIn or another similar tool. If you find you share something in common, when the time is right, mention it from your perspective, like, "When I worked at IBM . . ." and see if they take the bait. Then hope they say, "Wow, I also worked there . . . ." I am not saying be deceitful; I am simply saying do your homework and capitalize on what you actually have in common.

This "gift of gab," as my mother calls it, comes easily to some people but is very difficult for others. The good thing is your ability to become a conversationalist can improve through training, practice, and experience, just like building an under-used muscle. If you have not already done so, I would strongly suggest you study emotional intelligence, active listening, personal communication styles (like DISC or Merrill and Reid Social Styles), public speaking, storytelling, and other communication activities.

The following spreadsheet is a simple but structured way to list the people with whom you would like to create a closer professional bond. Record this information with the objective of enhancing your ability to influence them in the future if needed. We tend to do this mentally anyway. The power of writing it down, however, is that it gives structure to your thoughts. Also, by using an influence technique called "consistency," which you will learn about later in the book, you will be more likely to do it simply because you wrote it down.

Personal Connections Worksheet

People with Whom You Would Like to Create a Closer Bond	Reason to Connect	Notes

BARRIERS TO INFLUENCE

Generally speaking, people are not against you; they are for themselves.
Understand their reasoning and you can find strategies
to gain their support.

~ Eric Bloom

Throughout this book, I'll be talking about the importance of influence and how to use it tactically, strategically, and situationally. I will also provide you with what I hope you will find to be great concepts, tips, tricks, and measurements on how to use this influence. In this section, I would like to openly admit and state that, in many cases, influencing others is easier said than done.

When someone creates a barrier that blocks your way, such as refusing to sign a needed document, not responding to an important email, or not attending a long-scheduled meeting, it's natural to sit back and ask yourself one of the following questions:

- What am I doing wrong?

- Why doesn't this person like me?

- What does this person have against me?

PEOPLE ARE NOT AGAINST YOU; THEY ARE FOR THEMSELVES.

This is a key concept. It is important because it refocuses your attention to the other person, not yourself. If you understand why the other person believes what you are doing is not in their best interest, you can change your strategy or find another way to explain what you want to accomplish.

For example, if you are trying to implement new sales management software, you can explain it to the salespeople in one of two ways:

1. "This new sales management software will make you so efficient, we'll be able to raise your annual sales quotas."

2. "This new sales management software will increase your efficiency, allowing you to sell more products and increase your sales commission."

As you may expect, the salespeople will definitely dislike the first statement, but really like the second one.

Truly understanding your audience is key to influencing them.

BY DEFINITION, INFLUENCE FACILITATES CHANGE.

Continuing on the theme that it is about understanding your audience, you must understand what it is about the way you are trying to influence them that is causing them to resist. This resistance may be caused by one of the following factors:

- **Organizational Culture:** Your request is going against the grain of the organization's culture, goals, or direction.

- **Individual philosophy:** The person may have a different attitude toward the issue or think it should be solved in a different way.

- **General stagnation:** The person or organization may be stuck in their current way of doing things and not want to change, even if the change is in their best interest.

- **Perceived loss:** The person believes assisting in your initiative is in some way detrimental financially, politically, or otherwise.

- **Political infighting:** The people in your department do not get along with people in the other person's department. Organizational silos of this type are very detrimental to the overall organization and can stop your project dead in its tracks.

- **Lack of interest:** The person you are trying to influence has no vested interest in helping you, does not believe in your cause, or has no motivation to help you.

- **Disagreement with task or direction:** If the person understands what you are trying to do and does not like your direction, not only can they not be personally influenced, but they may try to persuade others not to follow you.

- **Poor communication:** People are not getting your message and/or are simply unaware that you are trying to influence them.

YES, IT MIGHT BE YOU.

Okay, yes. It could be you. Maybe you:

- Have not effectively explained your point of view.

- Have not thought through the ramification of what you are trying to do.

- Have not presented your idea in a way that relates to the person/people you are trying to influence.

- Are not liked by the person.

While these scenarios are unlikely, they are possible and should at least be considered.

THERE WAS A TIME WHEN THE BARRIER TO INFLUENCE WAS ME.

Many, many years ago, I was transferred to a new role setting up the supporting technology for a new business area. The manager of the business group I would be supporting seemed to hate me from the moment we met.

No, not hate—that's not a strong enough word. It was somewhere south of disdain. This was very scary to me because she would have significant input on my next performance review. I had many sleepless nights worrying that at some point I would lose my job.

About two weeks after our initial introduction and various uncomfortable discussions, I went into her office to apologize for whatever I had done to upset her. If effect, I was pleading to keep my job. When she saw me at her office door, it was clear that she did not want to talk to me. I immediately apologized and asked if we could please start over.

She looked down, laughed, and shook her head. At that moment, I was writing my resume in my head. She looked up and said that she owed me an apology. I looked at her surprised and said that I didn't understand. She said the reason she always looked at me with such disdain was I looked exactly like her ex-husband. We both laughed, and for the first time in weeks, I felt my job might still be secure.

We made a deal. She would try not to think of her ex-husband when she looked at me, and I would understand if she called me "Jeff" when we were arguing. I successfully supported the technological infrastructure of her department for about two years. Once this issue passed, she was great to work for, and I used her as a professional reference three or four years later.

The moral of this story is, at the end of the day, people are people. I got through this scenario by dumb luck. My hope for you is that you make your own luck by always remembering that to influence others, you must first understand their perspective. It is up to you to figure out "the why behind the what" and devise a plan to move forward.

Barriers to Influence Worksheet

Project/Initiative Name: _____

Who	Barrier Type	Notes/Actions

SEVEN KEY INFLUENCE STRATEGIES

Influence, like all other interpersonal skills, is something we have been doing by gut feel since taking our first breath. Studying influence-based concepts and techniques allows you to enhance your effectiveness through experience, practice, and algorithmical improvement.

~ Eric Bloom

As a CEO, department manager, or individual contributor, the ability to influence your peers, vendors, clients, and others is key to both your organization and your professional reputation.

When people think about influencing others, they often think about short-term tactics that are sales-like in approach and appearance. While these certainly are influence techniques, I would like you to widen your thinking and perspective on influence within the workplace and in general.

Below are seven key influence strategies that can be used alone or in combination to achieve your desired outcome.

STRATEGIC INFLUENCE

Strategic influence is a long-term, holistic approach to building the influence you would like to wield in the future. This could be leadership in a business, technical, or social arena. It could also be quietly and efficiently building credibility, connections, skills, knowledge, and/or infrastructure for use in the future.

Strategic influence may mean taking a leadership role in your company's digital strategy, business direction, and key internal projects, and/or implementing processes supporting a leading industry trend. This long-term, strategic influence not only builds your resume, but it enhances your professional brand as a business and technical leader.

Use strategic influence to:

- Create a personal career development plan.

- Lay the foundation for influencing specific people by performing specific actions now that will pay influential dividends later, such as:
  » Providing some assistance and/or minor favors.
  » Building relationships with those you would like to influence.
  » Increasing your subject-matter expertise.

TACTICAL INFLUENCE

Tactical influence uses specific, short-term, influenced-based tactics to gain the support of a specific person for a specific purpose.

Examples of tactical influence include:

- **Reciprocity:** Doing something nice for someone now with the hope/anticipation that they will return the favor when needed.

- **Liking:** Getting people in important decision-making roles to like you, thereby getting them to support you when important decisions arise.

- **Delegated authority:** Gaining the support of senior players, such as the CEO of your company, and using their approval and authority to influence others.

- **Proactive action:** Being seen as the person leading the charge on an important business issue, thus getting others within the company to rally around your cause.

- **Presentation excellence:** Being a great speaker when presenting your thoughts and proposals can be used to gain the support of others in the room.

- **Being calm:** If you have a reputation for being calm, thinking clearly during times of adversity, and solving difficult issues, people will turn to you when issues arise, enhancing your influence during times of trouble.

Use tactical influence to:

- Motivate your team.

- Gain the support of your peers and project stakeholders.

- Facilitate your image as an internal agent of change with the ability to lead business-driven initiatives.

SITUATIONAL INFLUENCE

The term "situational influence" is most commonly used in a marketing context and relates to influencing people to buy products. I describe situational influence in a business context as your knowledge of the topic under discussion and the audience with whom you're currently speaking.

In business, all influence is situational. Understanding your relative level of knowledge and control is key in assessing your ability to influence them. For example, a project manager has more influence over a team than over stakeholders. As a second example, a brain surgeon who has no knowledge of football has a high level of influence over patients but has very little influence when discussing the NFL with friends. This brain surgeon will, however, gain influence if the discussion turns to the long-term effects of sports-related concussions.

This concept of "situational influence" will be explained in greater detail in the chapter "Understanding Workplace Situational Influence."

Use situational influence to:

- Define the required level of preparation for an important meeting.

- Identify your relative organizational clout as compared to others.

- Gauge your ability to push your personal agenda and know when to back off.

SELF-HELP-BASED INFLUENCE

Self-help-based influence is allowing yourself to be influenced by another person specifically for your personal betterment. For example, you feel stressed at work or in life in general, so you "buy-in" to someone's relaxation philosophy, exercise program, diet regimen, or other activities. This can be of great value to you from a self-help perspective. Additionally, if you understand how this self-help dynamic works, you can use it on other people, to have them follow your philosophy, program, concept, or other activities.

You can use this influence to build your organizational clout by providing technology and business solutions that help others enhance their productivity, increase their professional stature, and enhance their business knowledge.

Use self-help-based influence to:

- Enhance your skills, knowledge, and wellbeing.

- Gain an understanding of how the self-help dynamic works so you can use it with other people.

- Increase your reputation as a thought leader and team player by helping others in this manner.

- Build feelings of loyalty and reciprocity in those you help.

INVERTED INFLUENCE

Inverted influence is the strategy where you seemingly allow yourself to be influenced by another person specifically to gain their attention, favor, trust, and support. I do not personally like this strategy because I consider it both manipulative and disingenuous, but it can be an effective strategy, nevertheless.

Use inverted influence to:

- Use your organizational clout and delegated authority to your advantage.

- Raise your organizational visibility.

- Position yourself for promotion or other professional gains.

Be careful using this strategy. If it backfires, you could dramatically hurt your organizational influence and your professional reputation.

UNINTENDED INFLUENCE

Sometimes you try to influence someone to do one thing, but they are so against it that they do the opposite, which can undermine your goal. At a macro level, you occasionally see this happen to people running for political office. The candidate says something to influence and rally supporters that has the unintended consequence of energizing and motivating the candidate's opposition.

In business, this generally falls under the category of "no good deed goes unpunished." The classic example is when IT tries to implement a new system without the support of the receiving department's manager.

Interestingly, this type of unintended influence can also be used to your advantage as a way to cancel or push forward projects when your efforts are not accepted or appreciated. When pushback comes from a given manager, simply lower the project's prioritization and reallocate the resources. If the executives above the dissenting manager want the system implemented, they will convince the manager for you. Then, if the project becomes reprioritized, the department manager will be less of a hurdle.

Use unintended influence to:

- Monitor when and why this happens to others and use it to your advantage.

- Protect yourself by understanding what is happening and using emotional intelligence and empathy to secure your position.

REVERSE INFLUENCE

Reverse influence, often called "reverse psychology," is when you try to influence someone to do something by telling them they cannot or should not do it.

This is best used to motivate a staff member. You say something like, "I don't think that will work, but you're welcome to try it and prove me wrong."

FINAL THOUGHT

These seven influence strategies each provide you with a conceptual arrow in your influence quiver. The advantage of studying influence strategies, techniques, and tactics is that, by using process-based influence techniques, you can improve them over time through practice and algorithmic improvement, rather than through gut feelings.

Key Influence Strategies Worksheet

Project/Initiative Name: _____

Strategy Type	Person/ Organization	Notes/Actions
Strategic Influence		
Tactical Influence		
Situational Influence		
Self-Help-Based Influence		
Inverted Influence		
Unintended Influence		
Reverse Influence		

PUSH/PULL INFLUENCE

You get more bees with honey than vinegar.

~Italian Proverb

Push and pull influence refers to two opposing influence types:

Push type influence: Urging or forcing a person or group to perform a task, rather than motivating them to comply or help.

Pull type influence: Attempting to motivate a person or group to want to comply or perform the task at hand.

At first glance, it may seem that *push* is bad and *pull* is good. However, they can both be good or bad depending on the tactics and desired outcome.

PUSH TYPE INFLUENCE

Push influence can take many forms. Some forms we all see and follow on a daily basis, some we choose to follow for our own wellbeing, and others we try to avoid because they attempt to force us where we do not want to go.

Some push influences include legal requirements, expert authority, industry standards, societal norms, and regulatory mandates. All these pushes are to keep us safe and healthy, but they are pushes nevertheless.

Examples of these types of push influences include:

- **Legal requirement:** When driving a car, you must stop at red lights and go on green lights. As an interesting aside, the societal norm in Massachusetts, where I live, is if the traffic light turns yellow, you accelerate through it before it turns red.

- **Expert authority:** Doctors instruct us what to eat, what medication to take, and other similar activities. We follow their instructions because we believe their recommendations are good for us.

- **Industry standards:** Companies can make light bulbs with any size base they wish, but if the base does not properly fit into any light fixtures, no one will buy them.

- **Societal norms:** People do not talk in movie theaters during the movie or they will be told by everyone else to be quiet.

- **Regulatory mandates:** All employees are told they must wash their hands after using the restroom. This requirement is clearly posted in all restrooms within the United States and in many other countries around the world.

As mentioned, push influences can also be sinister or even illegal. They include threats like losing your job, physical harm, canceled projects, reduced funding, increased costs, or the loss of privileges.

PULL TYPE INFLUENCE

Pull influences take the form of collaboration, vision, personal charisma, and using facts and logic to motivate people to act.

Examples of pull influences include:

- **Collaboration:** Asking an individual or group to work with you toward a common goal.

- **Vision:** Painting a picture of a desirable future outcome.

- **Personal charisma:** Using personal charm to influence desired actions.

- **Facts and logic:** Describing a situation using facts and logic with the goal of presenting a convincing argument.

- **Emotional appeal:** Using emotional stories, expressions, and words to invoke an emotional reaction that becomes the basis for action.

- **Taking Responsibility:** Proactively taking ownership of an issue or task that needs attention with the goal of motivating others to assist you in the task's completion.

- **Benefits over features:** Describing why something should be done—the benefits it provides—rather than the process to create it or specific items being created.

- **Mutual gain:** Framing the activity or task in a way that highlights the benefits for the person you are trying to influence.

PUSH/PULL CONCEPT APPLICATION

The power of this Push/Pull concept is it can be used to help decide which type of influence you would like to use to get the desired result.

Say you are a manager and two of the people on your team, Sandy Beach and Ima Storm, are continually arguing over an old issue that keeps surfacing and causing conflict. You, as the team leader, need to get this problem solved because their arguing is hurting department morale and reducing department productivity.

You initially decide to use a pull-type influence approach, explaining to each employee the importance of learning to get along for the sake of the department, their job performance, and their long-term career growth at the company. You know they are both smart, career-oriented people, and you feel this is the best approach to motivate them to resolve this conflict.

This approach seems to work for a few weeks, but then they are back to their bickering, each blaming the other for reigniting their argument.

This time, you decide to take a more systematic pull-oriented approach. Rather than trying to motivate them to get along using the intangible importance of harmony to their department and themselves, you resort to facts and logic related to productivity and performance statistics.

This second approach, again, seems to work for a short while; then old habits prevail.

Finally, you decide to take a more push-oriented approach. You tell both Storm and Beach if they do not find a way to resolve their differences, they will both lose their jobs.

The move from pull to push, in this case, was a type of escalation process with the goal of finally bringing peace—or at least civility—to the workplace.

Push Type Influence Worksheet

Project/Initiative Name: _____

Push Type	Person/ Organization	Notes/Actions
Legal requirement		
Expert authority		
Industry standards		
Societal norms		
Regulatory mandates		

Pull Type Influence Worksheet

Project/Initiative Name: _____

Pull Type	Person/ Organization	Notes/Actions
Collaboration		
Vision		
Personal charisma		
Facts and logic		
Emotional appeal		
Taking Responsibility		
Benefits over features		
Mutual gain		

INFLUENTIAL COMMUNICATION

*A powerful question, wrapped in a desirable future vision,
and enveloped in an emotionally charged story, can influence the world
to follow your direction.*

~Eric Bloom

Sometimes it is not what you say—it is how you say it, when you say it, where you say it, and/or the process you use to say it.

There are different techniques you can use in a seemingly ordinary conversation that dramatically enhance your ability to influence others. Your goal when experimenting with these techniques is to internalize them through practice, so using them does not seem calculated, disingenuous, or opportunistic.

The beauty of these techniques, in addition to their general applicability as an influence-based tactic, is that they are easily incorporated into other types of interactions, such as negotiation, conflict resolution, and delegation. Part 3 of this book provides insights into specific methods of incorporating these techniques into other activities.

While reading this chapter, you should consider the following questions:

- Which techniques do I like most and want to incorporate into my personal conversational repertoire?

- How do others use these techniques on me, and why do they work?

- How can I use these tactics in other interpersonal communications like negotiation and conflict resolution?

- Which tactics that I have observed others using would I like to use?

STORYTELLING

Using stories to convey information, maintain historical records, influence others, and perpetuate cultures, religions, and family identities is as old as humanity itself. Humans are internally wired to enjoy stories. Don't children want a bedtime story before going to sleep? Storytelling was the primary vehicle for passing information from generation to generation for a very long time.

Politicians often begin speeches by defining their accomplishments in terms of facts and figures. Then they try to humanize these accomplishments by telling a story about a specific individual, group, or municipality that benefited from their actions.

Storytelling, when done correctly, is so memorable because it brings together information, settings, actions, emotions, and other factors that stimulate different parts of the brain. As an example, have you ever said to yourself or others, "I don't remember what the speaker said, but I remember how they made me feel"?

How to tell a good story is outside the scope of this book. In fact, many books have been written with storytelling as the only topic. I suggest you study storytelling techniques via books, classes, YouTube videos, or other sources. When trying to influence others, storytelling will be of great value to you, and you will most likely have a little fun in the process.

PURPOSEFUL QUESTIONS

Asking the right type of question at the right time has great value, particularly if it is asked with a specific outcome in mind. The following purposeful question types allow you to lead individuals down a road they believe they are navigating.

These questions work so well because you are not telling people what to do; you are gently guiding them with the question in the direction you desire. Their internal thought process allows them to feel like they made the decision to move in the direction you desired. This makes it their idea, not yours.

Leading Questions

A leading question is posed with the intent of soliciting a specific outcome or action. For example, when a salesperson asks, "Do you have any more questions about the product before we start the paperwork?" what they mean is, "Okay, you have asked enough questions; let's sign the contract and move forward."

Other leading questions include:

- Honey, would you like chicken for dinner?

- Are there any more thoughts on this item before we move on to the next topic?

- Isn't this a great project plan?

- What can I do to be the best person for the job?

Descriptive Questions

The descriptive question provides information within the question. Using this type of question provides the advantage of telling people something without sounding pushy, disrespectful, self-serving, or boastful. In effect, you are sending a subliminal message in the form of a question.

For example, saying, "Our product has a really nice new video option. Have you tried it yet?" This example sounds friendly and inquisitive, and it contains a statement about your product combined with a leading question.

Other descriptive questions include:

- It rained last Friday. Did you have an umbrella?

- We have a very comprehensive data set. Do you think it would be worthwhile to try using predictive analytics as part of our next marketing plan?

Conversation Control Questions

This type of question is designed to gain permission to take control of the conversation. This question type can be used by many professions and in many circumstances. Business analysts, researchers, doctors, technical support personnel, and others can use this technique as a way to begin collecting the information needed to complete their task.

I personally use this type of question in two ways. First, when interviewing people for my blog, the conversation generally begins with the normal pleasantries, but at some point, the interview must start. Then I ask, "Is it okay with you if I go into interview mode and ask you a bunch of questions?" The answer is virtually always "Yes," and the interview begins. A second way I like to use this question type is to collect information for a custom class or keynote speech I am preparing for a client. I will ask, "May I ask you lots of questions to better understand your requirements and the audience's needs and interests?"

Other conversation control questions include:

- "I'm going to ask you a series of questions, okay?"

- "I can help you best if we stay on topic, agreed?"

MULTI-STEP COMMUNICATION

Multi-step communication consists of predefined processes crafted to create a specific response and/or outcome. This communication type is often used in conflict resolution, difficult conversations, change management, motivation, and other related activities. At their core, however, they are influence vehicles generic enough to be used in situations of all types.

Problem/Vision Statements

Within a business setting, this technique is primarily used to gain approval and/or funding for a specific project. The "problem statement" defines the issue that must be solved, and the "vision statement" describes the desired end-state once the problem has been corrected. The format for each statement is shown below:

Problem statement:
The problem is _____, resulting in _____, thereby causing _____.

Vision statement:
It would be great if _____, allowing us to _____, thereby having the effect of _____.

For example, if the VP of sales wants funding to upgrade the company's customer relationship management (CRM) system. The VP could say:

Problem statement:
The problem is *the CRM system is running slowly*, resulting in *inefficiencies in our sales process*, thereby causing *lower company revenue*.

Vision statement:
It would be great if *we upgraded the CRM software*, allowing us to *increase sales personnel efficiency*, having the effect of *increasing company revenue.*

The concept is that the problem causes feelings of anxiety and urgency, and the vision describes the problem-free future state. The trick is to get decision-makers to buy into the problem statement. Then it is easier to influence them to approve the funding or solution.

Fear/Protection

The Fear/Protection technique is used in business, politics, fundraising efforts, and other areas.

With this technique, you induce fear of a specific outcome with the goal of getting people to approve a project, vote for a specific candidate, or give money to a particular cause. A workplace example would be:

"Our competition is driving us out of business, and we're all going to lose our jobs if we don't increase our product quality. I can save us from this fate if you [desired action goes here].

Action/Consequences/Correction

This sequence is generally associated with difficult conversations, like an employee-performance issue. This issue could be ongoing or based on a single event.

The structure is:

Action: What the person did/is doing
Consequences: The problem it caused/is causing
Correction: The corrective action to be taken

In a business context, this three-step process can be used anywhere.

Example 1:

- **Action:** Low department funding

- **Consequences:** Overworked staff, reduced quality, increasing attrition

- **Correction:** Additional funding and hiring

Example 2:

- **Action:** Being rude to client

- **Consequences:** Loss of client, reduced company revenue

- **Correction:** Hold your temper when speaking to clients

Unfreeze/Transition/Refreeze

Kurt Lewin (1890 – 1947), a German-American psychologist, is considered one of the pioneers of applied psychology. He developed a three-step model for individual and organization change called Lewin's 3-Stage Model of Change:

Stage 1: Unfreezing—Creating the right conditions for change to occur

Stage 2: Changing—Beginning to resolve uncertainty and look for new ways to do things

Stage 3: Refreezing—Reestablishing a new place of stability and elevating peoples' comfort levels

This model is also applicable to influence because all influence creates change.

Statement Repetition

This technique is most often associated with two wildly different activities: difficult conversations and political rallies.

When used in difficult conversations, most often between manager and employee, the person leading the discussion repeatedly asks the same question until the other person answers the question.

For example, a discussion between a manager and an employee about the employee continually coming in late may have the following dialogue.

Manager: *How will you change your morning schedule so you will arrive at work on time?*

Employee: *It's not my fault; there's lots of traffic.*

Manager: *How will you change your morning schedule so you will arrive at work on time?*

Employee: *Even when the traffic is light, it's hard to find a parking space.*

Manager: *How will you change your morning schedule so you will arrive at work on time?*

Employee: *Okay, I'll leave my house earlier to get to work on time.*

In this dialogue, the manager keeps asking the employee the same question until the employee stops making excuses and eventually answers. The influence component is created because the manager does not give up until the employee commits to a workable solution.

This technique is also used in speeches at political rallies. Politicians often repeat the same words or phrases multiple times in their speeches to build momentum, increase energy, or create a memorable catch phrase.

LOGISTICAL ASSISTANCE

Certain places and times can affect when people are more likely to be influenced. These scenarios are described below.

Location Selection

At times, you can enhance your level of influence by controlling your physical location. For example, if you want to exert control over a meeting, meet in your office, not the other person's.

As an example, a salesperson may bring a client to a high-end restaurant, spend a lot of money on them, and then ask them to sign a contract. Or, a real estate agent has a very nice car to transport their clients from house to house. This shows the clients that the realtor is successful and ensures the clients are luxuriously comfortable and in no hurry to leave—unless, of course, they buy a house.

The concept of subtle, location-based influence can also be used within a room by sitting in the highest office chair so everyone has to look up to you, while you are looking down at them. Another technique of this type is to sit with your back to the window. If it's sunny out, others in the room must look slightly down to avoid the glare, but this is also submissive body language. This position, in turn, can slightly change their thought process and feeling of power.

Event End Timing

This technique is often used by fundraisers and keynote speakers. Fundraisers ask for money at the end of a great event or in the wake of a tragic incident. Speakers use this technique to sell products in the back of the room after giving a brilliant and motivational speech.

This technique works by influencing people to do something while they are at an emotional high or low in response to the event. These extremes make people more likely to act.

DIRECT REQUEST

Sometimes, the best way to influence someone is simply to ask for what you want directly. Examples of this in the workplace include:

- Would you please reply immediately to my email? I have a tight deadline.

- Could I please ask you for a favor?

- Would you please approve my project? I'll be happy to review the details first if you wish.

This direct method can work easily if you warm up the person first by subtly using another influence technique or two before "the ask."

As an example, let's say you want to ask Jessie to approve your project. First, find a way to do Jessie a small favor of some type. This creates a sense of obligation.

Alternatively, before asking Jessie, you could get a few other people to approve your project; ideally, people whom Jessie respects. This allows you to use three influence techniques simultaneously:

- Social proof (safety in numbers), because other people have signed it.

- Authority, because Jessie respects those who have already signed it.

- Liking, because if Jessie likes the other people who signed it, it's likely Jessie will want to go along with them.

Influential Communication Worksheet

Project/Initiative Name: _____

Communication Type	Person/ Organization	Notes/Actions
Storytelling		
Direct Request		
Purposeful Questions		
Leading Questions		
Descriptive Questions		
Conversation Control Questions		
Multi-Step Communication		
Problem/Vision Statements		
Fear/Protection		
Action/Consequences/ Correction		
Unfreeze/Transition/Refreeze		
Statement Repetition		
Logistical Assistance		
Location Selection		
Event End Timing		

WAYS TO SAY *NO* WITHOUT SAYING *NO*

Friends may come and go, but enemies accumulate.

~Thomas Jones (1892–1969)

Saying no is an often overlooked influence technique. It is not simply saying no; it's saying no and suggesting you or the other person/people involved do something differently. For example, someone asks you to give them a recap of a meeting they missed, but you don't have time to do so. Rather than just saying no, you could use a leading question, saying, "I'd like to help, but I'm afraid I might accidentally leave out an important point. Did you know that the meeting's minutes are available online in the meeting notes? Do you think it would be better to look there?" This type of technique has the dual benefits of saving you from having to spend time recapping the meeting and simultaneously redirects the person to a place where they can get the needed information.

Using these types of "redirection techniques" can save you from:

- Feeling confrontational by saying no.

- Agreeing to perform work you don't want to do.

- Wanting to help but not having the needed time, information, and/or resources to provide assistance.

Saying no shouldn't make you feel confrontational if you're doing it for the right purpose. There are very valid professional and organizational reasons to say no to requests from your coworkers. From a professional perspective, the reasons to say no include:

- When wanting to say yes just to be nice.

- When wanting to say yes to end the conversation, because the other person doesn't want to take no for an answer.

- It's against personal ethics.

- When it introduces unwanted personal/professional risk.

- If it's not in the direction you would like your career to progress.

- If you are already overworked and unable to take on additional tasks.

- If it's not in your best interest, and you don't see a "greater good" that overrides its lack of personal advantage.

It's even easier to justify saying no if the reasons are based on the organization's wellbeing. These reasons include:

- If it's against company policy.

- When it's not in the best interest of the company.

- When someone is trying to circumvent required/standard control processes.

- If it's a low priority, where time and money should be spent in other areas.

- Due to managerial instruction, when your manager told you to say no.

- If there is a negative return on investment (ROI) without a specific strategic decision to move forward, namely, the cost of implementing their request would be greater than the benefit it provides.

In addition to stopping bad things, saying no can result in many advantages, including:

- Allowing yourself more time to work on your most important projects.

- Helping to maintain work/life balance by not continually taking on more tasks.

- Enhancing your productivity by not performing superfluous tasks.

- The topics/techniques that follow are alternative ways to say no without actually saying no by either providing alternatives or redirecting the question.

SAYING NO USING REDIRECTION

This technique is best when you are willing to help but believe what they are asking you to do either won't work or you would rather do it a different way. In this case, your reply should provide an alternative solution, such as:

- I'm sorry I won't be able to help you with that, but perhaps I could....

- I don't think that will work, but....

- Have you considered this instead...?

- I'm afraid that won't work, but can I suggest....

SAYING NO BY REDIRECTING WORK BACK TO THE REQUESTOR

This technique is best when someone comes to you with a big idea for something they would like done but they want you to do all the work. In addition to the workplace, this often happens when you are in a volunteer role within a non-profit, religious, or other charitable organization. The person making the request is often a fellow volunteer or able-bodied recipient of the service.

When confronted with this type of request, respond with, "Interesting. Would you like to lead a volunteer committee to research this?" When posed with this question, one of two things will happen. The person will either agree to help, which is great, or will go away and leave you alone.

SAYING NO USING REFERRAL

This technique is best when you're willing to provide assistance, but someone other than you could do a better job, or you need permission to perform the task. In the first case, refer them to the person best able to assist them. In the second case, ask that they speak with your boss to gain permission. The following two replies can be used respectively:

- I'm not the best person to help on this. Can I suggest you speak with…?

- I'm happy to help you, but you'll have to get my boss' okay first.

SAYING NO USING THE COMPANY HIGH ROAD

This technique is best when you feel uncomfortable saying no but know you should. This technique allows you say no using the delegated authority of those higher than you within your organization. In other words, you are basically saying that you would like to help but can't. Therefore, they will go away disappointed but not mad at you because it was not your decision. The following examples can be used when this situation arises. Modify them based on your job type and the request made.

- Sorry; I'd love to help, but I've already promised to help on another project and don't have time to do both projects.

- Sorry; I'd love to help, but I'm spending all my time on the software for the company's new marketing initiative.

- Sorry; I can't. The CIO told me to spend as much time as possible on this new cloud-based project because it's really important to our new computing platform.

AVOIDING THE QUESTION

Sometimes the best way to say no is to make sure the question is never asked.

To avoid being asked the question at all, use a gatekeeper to keep people away. This is a common practice used by busy executives to reduce their level of distraction. Your gatekeeper could be an administrative assistant who screens your incoming calls and handles your schedule. If this isn't available to you, you can easily screen your own incoming calls via caller identification and send numbers/people you're not familiar with or would rather avoid to voice mail.

SAYING NO THROUGH PROCESS

At times, you may find yourself saying no to the same question repeatedly. The danger of this scenario is that it could hurt your professional reputation by making it look like you are not a team player. If this is happening to you, create a policy that says no or a prioritization process that always seems to place this type of request at the bottom of the list.

The logic behind this concept is it allows you to deflect the blame from yourself to the policy or a previously approved prioritization process. This technique sends people with redundant requests away disappointed but not mad at you.

SAYING NO USING LEADING QUESTIONS

Leading questions are questions that point the asker in a specified direction. In effect, you are telling them to do something, but because it's in the form of a question, it feels much softer and helpful, rather than confrontational. These examples can be modified based on your job type and the likely requests:

- Did you know that Pat is much more knowledgeable in that topic than I am?

- Did you know that this information is available online on the website?

- Did you know that the website does a great job describing the needed steps?

BEING VAGUE AND NONCOMMITTAL

This technique is used within many cultures as an acceptable way to say no. In effect, you are saying no by not saying yes. Examples of how to do this include:

- Hmmm, interesting. Let me think about it, and I'll let you know.

- I won't have the time for a month or two. Could you ask me again then?

- Those dates don't work for me. Can you please send me other potential dates?

- My calendar is already full, but if something opens up, I'll give you a call.

- I'd like to help you, but I don't know how. I'll call if I think of something good.

If you use this technique, be careful that the person doesn't misinterpret your comment and think you have agreed to assist them. If they do, it could very embarrassing for both you and requestor when the person returns looking for results.

As an additional point, it's important for you to understand that this cultural norm exists in case someone says this to you.

SAYING YES WITH CONDITIONS

This technique is best when you are willing to help but want either assistance or something specific in return. In this case, reply in the following way:

- Yes, but to make that work, I'll need....

- Yes, but I'll need help from Mary on....

- Yes, if you are willing to providing the following....

- Yes, if I can delay another required task such as....

- Yes, if I can...(get something of value out of it).

FINAL THOUGHT

Don't underestimate the importance of saying no in a non-offensive and constructive way. Over the course of your career, your professional reputation is not only defined by your achievements; it's also based on your willingness to help your coworkers and how you treated them during the process.

Ways to Say *No* Without Saying *No* Worksheet

Technique Type	How and when to use this technique to my advantage
Saying no using redirection	
Saying no by redirecting work back to the requestor	
Saying no using referral	
Saying no using the company high road	
Avoiding the question	
Saying no through process	
Saying no using leading questions	
Being vague and noncommittal	
Saying yes with conditions	

LEVELS OF COMMITMENT

Your influence-based activities, time, and effort should be spent on those who do not already agree with you; otherwise, you are simply irritating those who already support you.

~Eric Bloom

The ability to influence your coworkers is, of course, a very important skill. To maximize its effectiveness, however, you must also know whom to influence. The strategic ability to decide who, where, and when to influence allows you to prioritize your time, carefully use your political capital, and not accidently wear out your welcome.

To this end, the following worksheet (Figure 8.1) illustrates the intersection of people's commitment to your vision/project and the importance of their approval to your success. It is this intersection of commitment and need that defines the prioritization of those who must be influenced to meet your business objectives.

Enter the necessary names into the appropriate intersecting cells on the Commitment/Support Matrix (Figure 8.1) based upon their current commitment and your need. This gives you a visual representation of where to spend your influence-related energies.

The definition of each of the matrix values is listed below:

LEVELS OF COMMITMENT TO YOUR OBJECTIVE
The following describe people's various levels of commitment toward your project goal.

Commitment/Support Matrix

	Level of Support Needed				
	Must actively support	Must acquiesce	Can influence stakeholders	Has little influence	Has no influence
Committed					
Enrolled					
True compliance					
Compliance					
Reluctant compliance					
Apathy					
Non-compliance					

Level of Current Commitment

Figure 8.1

Committed: An advocate of your project

These people are great to have on your team because they believe in what you are trying to do and will provide whatever assistance is needed to help you succeed. However, it is important to know why they support you because you want to feed their enthusiasm to ensure they stay committed to your cause. You also must be very careful not to do anything that contradicts the reason for their support. The loss of a strong and visible advocate of your project can cause others to question their own support, particularly if this person is highly respected by your other supporters.

Enrolled: Will invest time to help facilitate your project's success

These people will provide assistance, support, and funding when asked, but your project will not be a top priority. These could be people who generally support your work, have a small vested interest in your project, or think your project is good for the company and, therefore, merits their support.

True compliance: Willing to comply with the spirit of your project

These people will follow instructions and wish you well. They may also provide you with input and suggestions, if asked. Their willingness to happily comply may be for one of the following reasons:

- They like you and want to be of help.

- They agree that the initiative will be good for the organization and, thus, want to participate.

- They think the initiative will be good for them and provide personal advantage.

- They have a high respect for authority and will follow directions if asked.

Properly understanding the "who" behind their willingness to comply gives you insight into how to potentially elevate their support to enrolled or committed.

Compliance: Will do what is required without complaint

Those falling into this category believe that your project will cause them neither pleasure nor pain. As a result, they see no benefit or risk in following your request. The danger of people in this category is they are more likely to drop down toward noncompliance than up toward commitment. You want to gently move them toward your goal without pushing them too hard or causing them any difficulty.

Reluctant compliance: Will do the minimum to avoid trouble

People with this attitude toward your project have no vested interest in your work or you in general. Although they don't wish you harm, they will not do any more than the minimum required. This level of commitment from a single individual is generally not an issue. However, if you need their support or their team's resources, their stance can easily become problematic.

Apathy: Do not care about you or your project; do as they're told

As the title of this category suggests, people who are apathetic toward you or your project are putting forth a quiet reluctance. At best, they want no involvement or connection to your project; at worst, they will block your way through a combination of inaction and unfulfilled promises.

Noncompliance: Will not comply with your requests and will actively work to undermine you

These people want your project to fail. The reason behind this animosity could be personal, but it is more likely that there is something about your project they dislike for one of the following reasons:

- They conceptually believe you are moving in the wrong direction.

- They feel your success will hurt them in some way, such as reduced income, lower professional stature, or stunted career growth.

- They have a personal or departmental goal that is in direct conflict with what you are trying to accomplish. Thus, if you are successful, their project will be hurt.

If there are people within your company who fall into this noncompliance category, your first step is to understand the reason behind their noncompliance. Upon doing so, one of the following plans of action may be of value:

- Listen to why they disagree with you. If they think you are going in the wrong direction, maybe you are and have not seen it. Be flexible if they are right.

- If you do not believe your project will be a problem for them, have a discussion with them to address their concerns. You may be able to find middle ground with an acceptable compromise.

- If you cannot reach an agreement, at least try to "agree to disagree" on direction and principle. Then attempt to find a way you can both move forward without hurting each other's interests.

REQUIRED LEVELS OF SUPPORT BY SPECIFIC INDIVIDUALS

Whereas the level of commitment measures the willingness of people to support your project, the level of need measures the importance of their support in moving your project forward. In effect, the commitment level is what they think of you, and the level of need is what you think about them.

Must actively support: Without full commitment, your project will fail

The support of these people is essential for you to be successful. Your project will fail without their approval, resources, budget, or other key components. For example, if you are trying to implement a customer resource management (CRM) system with a sales organization, the VP of sales must support the project. Even if the system is implemented, it will not be adopted by the salespeople if the VP does not require them to make the change.

Must acquiesce: You need their approval but not their ongoing support

This category of people cannot necessarily help you succeed, but they can make you fail. For example, if you are in a regulated industry, such as financial services or healthcare, you may need the approval of the compliance and/or legal departments to proceed. As a second example, if you want to implement a new employee goal-setting process within your department, it would be nice to have the help of the human resources (HR) group to use their expertise in employee performance measurement. Even if they are not willing to help you with implementation, their approval may be required because of HR's political clout within your organization.

Can influence stakeholders: Has no direct control but can influence needed decision makers

Those who fall into this category do not have any direct control over you or your projects; however, they have the ability to influence those who do. These people are generally in one of the following organizational roles:

- Staff-type job, such as strategic planning, reporting to the decision maker.

- Friend or relative of the decision maker who can influence decisions related to your project.

- Stakeholder with organizational clout who will be affected by your project.

- Person partially or fully funding the project.

Has little influence: Has no direct ability to influence decision makers but can raise issues about your project if unhappy

This person has very little actual influence, but thinks they do. They will have to work hard to get the ear of the decision maker, but it is possible if they feel strongly for or against your project. Minimally, they can be a minor player singing your praises or an annoyance who could cost you time, money, and aggravation.

Has no influence: Has no effect on your project

Lastly, people in this category have no internal political clout and, theoretically, have no effect on your project's success or failure. Beware, the danger with people in this category is the unknown. For example, what if the high school intern opening envelopes in the accounts receivable department is the daughter of the chief financial officer (CFO), and you don't know it?

THE INFLUENCE PRIORITIZATION PROCESS

Step 1: Complete the Commitment and Required Support Matrix

At first glance, you may think there is no real value in completing this worksheet because you already know the players, their interest in helping you, and the organizational landscape regarding who can help or hurt your project.

The importance of completing this worksheet is twofold. First, it makes you sit down and focus on each person individually, which increases your understanding of those around you. Second, a graphic representation of all this information makes it easier to conceptually analyze your overall political landscape.

The Example Commitment and Required Support Matrix (Figure 8.2) illustrates a completed Matrix for a new accounts receivable system within the finance department.

Those named in Figure 8.2 have the following roles:

Pat: Manager of accounts receivable (AR)
Morgan: Newly hired staff accountant
Jesse: Chief financial officer (CFO)
Avery: Legal council
Jean: VP of risk management
Shawn: Senior cash flow analyst

When reviewing the matrix (Figure 2), note that Jean, VP of risk management, is **Must Actively Support and Non-Compliant.**

Example Commitment and Required Support Matrix

	Level of Support Needed				
	Must actively support	Must acquiesce	Can influence stakeholders	Has little influence	Has no influence
Committed	*Pat*				*Morgan*
Enrolled		*Jesse*			
True compliance					
Compliance		*Avery*			
Reluctant compliance					
Apathy					
Non-compliance	*Jean*		*Shawn via Pat*		

Level of Current Commitment

Figure 8.2

Jean:

Must actively support: Without full commitment, your project will fail

The support of these people is essential for you to be successful. Your project will fail without their approval, resources, budget, or other key components.

Noncompliance: Will not comply with your requests and will actively work to undermine you

These people want your project to fail. The reason behind this animosity could be personal, but it is more likely that there is something about your project they dislike.

So, given Jean's position in the company and on the matrix, it is clear that you must convince Jean that the new accounts receivable system and process are good for the company. The first question in defining your influence plan for Jean is to understand her lack of support for your project. You may find that new reports need to be generated, your implementation process may need to be documented better, or maybe Jean just needs to be more carefully included in project communications. In any case, Jean is clearly your first priority.

The commitment levels for Pat, manager of AR, and Jesse, CFO, may seem backwards, based upon their job titles.

Pat:

Must actively support: Without full commitment, your project will fail

The support of these people is essential for you to be successful. Your project will fail without their approval, resources, budget, or other key components.

Committed: An advocate of your project

These people are great to have on your team because they believe in what you are trying to do and will provide whatever assistance is needed to help you succeed.

Jesse:

Must acquiesce: You need their approval, but not their ongoing support

This category of people cannot necessarily help you succeed, but they can make you fail.

Enrolled: Will invest time to help facilitate your project's success

These people will provide assistance, support, and funding, when asked, but your project will not be a top priority. These could be people who generally support your work; have a small, vested interest in your project going well; or think your project is good for the company and, therefore, merits their support.

In this case, however, Pat has been given the authority (delegated authority) by Jesse to make decisions on the new AR system. Jesse must agree, but Pat is driving the process. Therefore, the best way to get Jesse to acquiesce is to get Pat to actively support your solution.

Also take note that while Shawn, the senior cash flow analyst, does not have direct decision-making authority over your project, Shawn can influence Pat, who must be on your side. Therefore, working to get Shawn on your side is time well spent.

Shawn:

Can influence stakeholders: Has no direct control but can influence needed decision makers

Those who fall into this category do not have any direct control over you or your projects; however, they have the ability to influence those who do.

Noncompliance: Will not comply with your requests and will actively work to undermine you

These people want your project to fail. The reason behind this animosity could be personal, but it is more likely that there is something about your project they dislike.

FINAL THOUGHT

When you take the time to enter the information into the matrix, you will notice the organizational nuances presented in a graphic manner. These nuances can make the difference between your project's success and failure. Knowing how to prioritize your influence and political capital is priceless.

CIALDINI'S SIX PRINCIPLES OF PERSUASION

Often, we don't realize that our attitude toward something has been influenced by the number of times we have been exposed to it in the past.

~Robert B. Cialdini, *Influence: The Psychology of Persuasion*

Robert B. Cialdini, PhD, author of *Influence: The Psychology of Persuasion*, inspired me to learn more about influence and eventually to pursue my own influence-related research. My goal in this chapter is to give you a basic understanding of Cialdini's six ways to influence others. For a deeper understanding of his research and conclusions, I strongly suggest that you read his book.

As you review these six influence types, try to expand your thoughts beyond the technique itself and consider its potential application within your business environment. To assist you in the process of integrating these techniques into your workplace, Part 3 of this book discusses how these and other techniques can enhance your success when negotiating, resolving conflict, selling, delegating, implementing change, and other related workplace activities.

RECIPROCITY

The concept of reciprocity is the desire to return a favor and treat others as you have been treated. Therefore, when you do something nice for someone, if given the opportunity, they will feel obliged to do something nice for you.

As a fun example, assume that you and I live in the same neighborhood and every summer your family has a big party. However, you have never invited my family to attend. I could just ask you to invite us, but I don't feel comfortable taking that approach. Instead, I invite your family to my first annual winter holiday party. Whether or not you attend my holiday party, the invitation causes you to feel obligated to reciprocate with an invitation to your next summer party.

COMMITMENT/CONSISTENCY

This concept illustrates that people, by their nature, want to be consistent. Therefore, once someone commits to something, they are more inclined to do it again. That is why when you get a call from a charity to which you previously donated, the caller begins the conversation by thanking you for your previous donation.

From a business perspective, you can strategically use this concept when you know you need substantial future support by asking for something small now. In the interim, you may also consider using other types of influence, like building your "Reciprocity Bank." By doing things for a person, such as offering your department resources to help them, you build in them a feeling of obligation (reciprocity) to help you in the future.

SOCIAL PROOF (SAFETY IN NUMBERS)

We can view Social Proof in two ways. First, people often look at others' behavior for direction on choices. For example, a company is more likely to buy a product that all their major competitors purchase than a product that is unknown within their industry. Second, there is safety in numbers. A decision has a lower business risk if the same decision has been made by others within the same department or company.

LIKING

We see this concept in practice almost every day. People are more likely to be influenced by people they like. Consider your own experience. Whose advice are you more likely to take: a friend's, a stranger's, or a person you know but dislike? People are, generally, more successful in jobs when people like them. Therefore, from a business perspective, not only is it more fun to work with people you like and who like you, but it also increases the potential for professional success.

AUTHORITY

It is easier to persuade others if you are recognized as an expert or organizational authority. For example, if you work in a heavily regulated industry, like financial services, healthcare, or medical devices, the compliance department represents an expert authority even if they have no direct connection to your project.

You can use this concept to your advantage by positioning yourself as an authority. As an expert, it is easier for you to influence your coworkers. For example, if you are certified in project management, all other things being equal, you are in a position of authority over those who are not certified. This same concept is true for certifications, degrees, professional experience, awards, and/or other business accomplishments.

SCARCITY

The concept of scarcity is rather interesting. The principle of scarcity states things are more attractive when their availability is limited or we believe we may lose the opportunity to acquire them. So, a special offer that expires at midnight, while supplies last, is intended to motivate consumers to act because they don't want to lose out.

Study after study validates that, as a motivator, the fear of loss is greater than the desire for gain. For example, you find a potential new hire you like, but you do not present the offer immediately. Then the potential employee calls to let you know they have another offer in hand. Your fear of losing the opportunity to hire this person motivates you to complete the paperwork quickly so you can present the job offer.

BRINGING IT ALL TOGETHER, EXAMPLE

Thus far, we discussed each of these six influence types individually. The Quality Value Convenience (QVC) TV channel is masterful at combining multiple forms of influence to persuade you to buy their products. If you are not familiar with QVC, they offer retail products that you can purchase by phone or online via demonstrations on their TV channel.

QVC combines influence techniques in various ways, including the following:

- **Authority:** A person perceived as an expert explains the benefits of the product.

- **Liking:** Instead of an authority, they might use a celebrity spokesperson whom people like and trust to describe the product. The idea is to make you think: Wow, they star in one of my favorite movies. This product must be really good. I think I'll buy one.

- **Social Proof (Safety in Numbers):** While they talk about the product on air, they display the number of people who have ordered the product—ten products sold . . . twenty products sold . . . thirty products sold—because they want you to say to yourself, "Wow, if all of these people are buying it, it must be really good!" They also take live calls from customers purchasing the product so you can identify with them.

- **Scarcity:** QVC, and other channels like it, display the number of products available, constantly updating how many remain for sale—only 100 left . . .only ninety left—as the product becomes increasingly scarce, they create a sense of urgency for the viewer to purchase before it is gone "forever."

Please note: I have no connection with QVC or any similar network and have never spoken with anyone there regarding their procedures, influence techniques, or selling processes. My thoughts about QVC's use of the principles of influence to persuade viewers is strictly based on my own observations while watching their channel.

Cialdini's Six Principles of Persuasion Worksheet

Project/Initiative Name: _____

Influence Type	Person or Situation	Notes/Actions
Reciprocity		
Commitment/Consistency		
Social Proof		
Liking		
Authority		
Scarcity		

COHEN-BRADFORD INFLUENCE CURRENCIES

Influence is possible when you have what others want.

~Allan R. Cohen and David L. Bradford

As previously mentioned, Robert Cialdini inspired me to study influence. Two others who inspired me are Allan R. Cohen and David L. Bradford, authors of Influence Without Authority. As with Cialdini's book, I strongly suggest you read Cohen and Bradford's book.

From my perspective, the Cohen-Bradford Model can best be described by the quote at the beginning of this chapter and the two quotes below:

"Influence is based on exchange and reciprocity, making trades for what you desire in return for what the other person desires."

"The metaphor of currencies, which stands for something that is valued, can help you determine what you might offer a potential ally in exchange for cooperation."

Cohen and Bradford's quote, *"Influence is possible when you have what others want,"* is, in my eyes, one of the most important quotes related to influence ever written. To use this quote to your advantage, you first need to determine what the other person wants and then provide it.

Cohen and Bradford define five categories of "currencies" to assist in categorizing the other person's wants. At first, currencies may make you think of money, which a currency could be, but it could also be so much more.

As you read through this list, think of the people you must influence today, or in the near future, and try to decide which of the influence currencies would work best for each individual.

INSPIRATION-RELATED CURRENCIES

These currencies are of value to those who are looking for a vision to follow and/or wish to make a positive difference for their department, their company, and/or the world. This category includes:

- **Vision:** Being involved in a task that has larger significance for your unit, organization, customers, or society.

- **Excellence:** Having an opportunity to do important things really well.

- **Moral/Ethical correctness:** Doing what is "right" based on a higher standard.

TASK-RELATED CURRENCIES

Sometimes people are willing to help you, but they don't have the time, money, resources, or knowledge necessary. This category of currencies is best described as "help them help you." If you are able to provide the resources needed for them to assist you, then they can use those resources on your behalf to help you meet your goals. These resource types include:

- **Additional resources:** Obtain money, budget increases, personnel, etc.

- **Needed learning:** Gain the skills needed to perform the task.

- **General assistance:** Receive help with existing projects or unwanted tasks.

- **Organizational support:** Receive overt or subtle backing or direct assistance with implementation.

- **Rapid response:** Get something quickly, such as budget, people, etc.

- **Information:** Gain access to organizational or technical knowledge.

POSITION-RELATED CURRENCIES

These currencies relate to people's internal need for belonging, the respect and recognition of others, or enhancement of their personal community. Some people require this type of reinforcement to reduce their own self-doubt or increase their self-esteem. Others require this form of reinforcement as a means-to-an-end, namely, as a stepping stone to enhance their career. These currency types include:

- **Recognition:** Acknowledgment of effort, accomplishment, or abilities.

- **Visibility:** Opportunity to be known by higher-ups or other significant players in the organization.

- **Reputation:** Being seen as competent and committed.

- **Insiderness/Importance:** A sense of centrality or belonging.

- **Contacts:** Opportunities to link with others.

RELATIONSHIP-RELATED CURRENCIES

These currencies are needed by people who want to be heard and/or build friendships inside and outside of the workplace. These currencies include:

- **Understanding:** Have concerns and issues listened to.

- **Acceptance/Inclusion:** Feel closeness and friendship.

- **Personal Support:** Receive personal and emotional backing.

PERSONAL-RELATED CURRENCIES

These currencies are for people who like to feel appreciated, avoid conflicts, and/or want to feel ownership of the endeavors in which they are involved.

- **Gratitude:** Appreciation or expression of indebtedness.

- **Ownership/Involvement:** Ownership of and influence over important tasks.

- **Self-Concept:** Affirmation of values, self-esteem, and identity.

- **Comfort:** Avoidance of hassles.

FINAL THOUGHT

Each time I review these five types of influence currencies, I am reminded that the primary way to influence others is to have empathy for them and understand their motivations and needs. Then, develop a specific influence strategy based on that person's needs. Influencing others is not about you; it's about them.

Before personally studying influence, I most often tried to influence others by using techniques that would work on me. One of the biggest lessons I've taken from Cohen-Bradford is that influencing others is not about what I want or need; it is about identifying and providing what they want or need so they will follow my vision.

Cohen-Bradford Influence Currencies Worksheet

Project/Initiative Name: _____

Currency Type	Person	Notes/Actions
Inspiration-Related Currencies		
Vision		
Excellence		
Moral/ethical correctness		
Task-Related Currencies		
Additional resources		
Needed learning		
General assistance		
Organizational support		
Rapid response		
Information		
Position-Related Currencies		
Recognition		
Visibility		
Reputation		

Currency Type	Person	Notes/Actions
Inspiration-Related Currencies (con't)		
Insiderness/Importance		
Contacts		
Relationship-Related Currencies		
Understanding		
Acceptance/Inclusion		
Personal Support		
Personal-Related Currencies		
Gratitude		
Ownership/Involvement		
Self-Concept		
Comfort		

ACTION/REACTION INFLUENCERS

For every action, there is an equal and opposite reaction.

~Isaac Newton's Third Law of Motion

One of my favorite ways to influence others is to perform a task that needs to be done anyway and to do it a manner that causes the other person to react in a specific way.

For example, if you need someone to respond to your emails more quickly, try responding to their emails quickly with the hope that they will return the favor.

I worked with a senior manager who took two or three days to respond to my emails. This was problematic because I was under a tight deadline and could not move forward without the manager's input on certain aspects of the project. In an attempt to speed up his replies, I would answer his messages within five or ten minutes. Because I always replied to his email messages right away, over time, he felt guilty that he did not do the same for me. As a result of this guilt, he began to return my email messages as soon as they arrived. Truth be told, this story falls under the category of: If you can't be smart, be lucky. Initially, I started responding to his emails so quickly because I thought he would email back right away if I could catch him while he was still working on email. It wasn't until weeks later that he realized his change was an influence-based reaction to my action. I got the result I wanted, but not for the reason I expected. I had no idea I was making him feel guilty about his slow replies. I thought he was simply still in the process of returning emails. Live and learn.

This is an example of the action/reaction influence concept. It does not always work, but over time, I've found it has a high winning percentage.

The beauty of this concept is that I had to write the email anyway, so all I did was strategically change the timing. Like this example, virtually all the techniques discussed in this chapter take very little or no additional effort, just strategic intent.

Additional action/reaction tactics are listed below.

STARTING MEETINGS ON TIME

Starting your meetings on time, even if all participants are not present, has many non-influence benefits, including:

- Allowing more time to get things done (a full sixty minutes for a one-hour meeting).

- Providing the opportunity to end the meeting early, giving participants a few minutes of the day back or to get to their next meeting.

- Illustrating your personal timeliness.

- Showing your respect for the people who show up on time.

From an influence perspective, your action of starting the meeting on time causes the following reactions:

- Influences people to be on time for your meetings because they feel uncomfortable joining a meeting after it has already begun.

- Influences people to complete their deliverables/tasks on time because you have a reputation for being timely.

- Assures willingness to attend your meetings because people know the meeting will start on time and possibly end early.

ACCEPTING CONSTRUCTIVE FEEDBACK

Your willingness to solicit and accept feedback from others has many business advantages, including:

- Gaining insight into how others judge your work.

- Gaining deeper understanding of your clients' current and future needs.

- Showing your strength of character by illustrating your willingness to listen to others.

- Illustrating your responsiveness in correcting issues and/or taking advantage of previously unseen business opportunities.

From an influence perspective, your action of soliciting and accepting constructive feedback, and exhibiting your willingness to correct your shortcomings, also causes the reaction of making other people, including your staff, more willing to accept constructive feedback from you.

OVERCOMMUNICATING

If you have staff, stakeholders, vendors, senior managers, or others who do not provide you with the information and/or communication you need to get your job done, the action of overcommunicating with them to provide the data they need causes the reaction of making them feel guilty for not communicating their information to you. These feelings will, hopefully, cause them to be more communicative.

PROVIDING DELIVERABLES EARLY

Business advantages exist for completing and providing your deliverables a little early, including:

- Being seen as a dependable business partner.

- Reducing personal stress related to last minute sprints to complete assignments.

- Illustrating your time-management capabilities and organizational skills.

- Reducing stress and uncertainty for those who cannot accomplish their work until they receive your deliverables.

From an influence perspective, your action of completing your tasks early causes the following reactions:

- More business leaders and peers want to work with you.

- Your consistently early completion of deliverables, especially those that pass back-and-forth with another party, helps push others to get their work done on time.

DOING TASKS YOU DON'T LIKE

As a leader, if you do all the fun stuff and leave the important but uninteresting or dangerous tasks to others, many issues will arise, including:

- Your team will resent you.

- Your staff will be unwilling to perform unwanted tasks.

- Your team's motivation will be reduced, resulting in lower productivity and increased attrition.

Your action of sharing the uninteresting or dangerous tasks has the reaction of:

- Showing people you are a team player, thus, increasing their willingness to follow your instruction.

- Causing your team (and others) to perform these tasks more willingly because they know you won't ask them to do anything you wouldn't do yourself.

TAKING LOGISTICAL CONTROL

Taking logistical control is a negotiation trick that employs both influence and team-building-based concepts. From an influence perspective, being proactive and organizing the group's logistical needs positions you to take a leadership role in the overall negotiation process. From a team-building perspective, once you have taken a leadership role and the group's culture is formed, modifying that culture becomes very difficult, thus cementing your role as the overall negotiation leader.

Continuing with the negotiation example (described in greater detail in Chapter 21: Influence-Based Negotiation), if you take care of the negotiation's logistics, such as booking the conference room, sending out the meeting invitations, and ordering lunch, the group will be more likely to follow your direction regarding negotiation-related items.

PAYING VENDORS QUICKLY

Prompt payment helps you maximize attention, support, and influence over your vendors. Paying your vendors quickly (even immediately, if possible) is especially effective with smaller vendors who are very attuned to their cash flow and accounts receivable. In short, the faster you pay them, the more likely they are to prioritize your work because they know payment will be immediate. This gives you a huge advantage over those who pay vendors in thirty or sixty days.

SAYING "THANKS AND YOUR THOUGHTS?"

When you ask a question within an email, how you end your email can significantly affect the number of replies and responses to your question. Use the action of soliciting an email response by ending your email with something like:

Thanks, and your thoughts?

Eric

This closing causes the reaction of increasing the likelihood of people replying to your email for the following reasons:

- People don't often read an entire email; therefore, if your question is in the middle, they may not see it.

- When they read your closing, they may feel uncomfortable not answering the question.

People are more likely to respond when you ask for their thoughts, rather than asking them to please reply or thanking them in advance for their response because you are asking, not telling. Also, by asking for what you want (their thoughts), it is easier for them to form a reply.

USING BODY LANGUAGE TO YOUR ADVANTAGE

The most commonly known example of the cause/effect phenomenon of body language is yawning—when someone yawns, it causes other people to yawn. Less known, but still prevalent, is that when someone clears their throat, you will often hear others clear their throats as well.

You can use body language to influence others in various ways.

First, you can use body language to affect people's perception—their perception can change their reaction toward you and your project.

From a business perspective, if you smile, it may influence the other person to smile. If you appear excited and involved, others may feel excited and involved. As humans, our actions affect others. The more we understand how our body language can influence others, the more we can use it to our advantage.

Second, it is human nature to make decisions about someone's level of confidence, abilities, and personal power by observing their body language. You can use this concept to influence how people think of you. If you want people to perceive you as confident and in charge, then stand up straight, keep your head up, walk with conviction, and exhibit traits that show strength.

This is a simple glimpse into the power of body language and how it can be used to your advantage. If I have piqued your interest, there are many books, classes, YouTube videos, and other resources to expand your knowledge.

Action/Reaction Influencers Worksheet

Project/Initiative Name: _____

Action/Reaction Influencers	Person/ Organization	Notes/Actions
Starting meetings on time		
Accepting constructive feedback		
Overcommunicating		
Providing deliverables early		
Doing tasks you don't like to do		
Taking logistical control		
Paying vendors quickly		
Saying "Thanks, and your thoughts?"		
Using body language to your advantage		

BUILDING AN INFLUENTIAL PROFESSIONAL BRAND

Your professional brand is defined by the opinion of others, because for them, their perception is their reality, regardless of your intent or best efforts.

~Eric Bloom

The stronger your professional brand, the greater your influence. This statement is true because people are more willing to take advice, suggestions, and directions from those they respect and admire. This chapter covers fifteen actions specifically designed to increase your influence by increasing your reputation.

PROVIDE EXECUTION EXCELLENCE

Being a top performer is a key component in gaining the respect of your peers. In many ways, an office has the same familiarity and many of the same dynamics as a family. Over time, your coworkers will know your strengths, weaknesses, ability to meet deadlines, how hard you work, if you're a team player, your problem-solving skills, the quality of the work you produce, and many other related items. These attributes combine to define your internal reputation and, thus:

- How much respect you command.

- How able and willing you are to help others.

- How much potential for upward mobility you have.

The better your coworkers feel about you regarding these three personal traits, the easier it will be for you, thus defining your ability to influence them.

Think of it from your perspective. Who would you follow at work—a top performer who is highly respected or a person known for low quality work and a lack of motivation?

Also, if you are viewed as upwardly mobile, people will want to be on your good side because you may be their boss in the future.

BE PROACTIVE

Being reactive is performing tasks upon request. While being reactive is of great importance, it is not enough. Being reactive makes you a follower, not a leader.

To be proactive:

- Show initiative.

- Seek client opinions regarding enhancing of service quality.

- Discover what new services are needed and move toward their implementation.

- Discontinue services that are no longer needed.

- Provide thought leadership by suggesting creative solutions and identifying potential new opportunities without the specific instruction to do so.

Being proactive is a combination of recognizing what must be done, having the motivation and the courage to take it on, and then being accountable for the results, good or bad. This is the essence of leadership. Proactive leadership allows you to lead and influence others through your commitment and conviction.

USE STRATEGIC RECIPROCITY

Reciprocity, as described in the previous chapter on Cialdini, states that people generally return favors and treat others as they have been treated. This inclination leads to a feeling of obligation to return the favor.

Strategic reciprocity is the process of creating a list of people you may need a favor from in the future. Then you strategically build your "reciprocity bank" with good deeds, so you can cash in a favor when needed.

To do this correctly, you cannot connect your previous good deeds to your current request. If you do, you create the potential for resentment and suspicion toward your previous actions.

Lastly, if you are going to do something nice for someone, do it for the right reasons. As members of the human community, we should help each other because it's the best way to be. That said, directing some of your altruistic nature toward those who can help you in the workplace is good business.

PROVIDE THOUGHT LEADERSHIP

Vertical knowledge is being a subject matter expert (SME) in a specific area, for example in website design. Horizontal knowledge is understanding how a specific technology or process is used across a wide variety of industries or professions. Thought Leadership is having the ability to combine your vertical and horizontal knowledge in innovative ways and to be willing to share it with others.

Sharing your cross-industry, horizontal knowledge and insights on how to move forward with new initiatives and technologies with others positions you as an agent of change and an organizational visionary.

TALKING ABOUT BENEFITS, NOT FEATURES

"Benefits" are the value received by an action, activity, or product. For example, the activity of exercising has the benefit of better health. Continuing this example, "Features" are the specific exercises that would be performed. As a second example, Microsoft Word has various features, such as a spell check, fonts, bolding text, etc. The "benefit" of Microsoft Word is the ability to create professional quality documents.

Experts have the ability to connect features to the benefits they provide. Non-experts often can't make this connection and/or don't care about the features.

Talking to people (management, stakeholders, customers, and others) in their language about benefits, not features, enhances your credibility and understandability, thus, increasing your influence.

HAVE AND SHOW STAKEHOLDER EMPATHY

Understanding the needs, wants, and interests of others allows you to:

- Anticipate their needs more accurately.

- Gain their respect.

- Speak their language.

- Gain their support.

- Receive their cooperation.

These attributes are of great value when trying to influence others. They create the basis for trust and provide the information needed to understand the easiest ways to influence others.

TAKING THE MORAL HIGH GROUND

Taking the moral high ground is a great influence and negotiation tool because it is hard for people to disagree with doing "the right thing for the right reasons." Taking this moral high ground also illustrates your ethics and commitment to the company, which further enhances your influence.

SHOW GRATITUDE

People appreciate being appreciated. Saying thank you when receiving assistance makes people want to provide you with additional assistance. Thanking people for their efforts also increases your likeability, which increases your ability to influence them.

ILLUSTRATE ORGANIZATIONAL AWARENESS

Truly understanding how to navigate organizational silos, prickly personalities, bureaucratic paperwork, and other internal hurdles has multiple professional advantages, including:

- Avoiding political landmines.

- Fostering a reputation for being able to get things done.

- Building reciprocity by helping others attain their goals through providing advice and helping them navigate organizational bottlenecks.

PASSION AND CONVICTION

When people are passionate and have strong convictions about a topic, concept, activity, or objective, it is infectious and others want to follow them. This is how entrepreneurs get people to work for them for low wages, with only the promise of future riches. It is also why a charismatic and committed leader of a charity, non-profit, religious institution, or social cause can get people to volunteer their time and/or give their money to forward the cause.

BE A PROBLEM SOLVER

People's professional reputations are made and lost over their ability to solve problems. On the downside, the inability to solve a business issue under your watch is viewed as incompetency. On the upside, however, solving a major issue illustrates your coolness under pressure, analytical skills, creativity, and leadership. It also has the advantages of:

- Making you the "go to" person when problems arise.

- Getting yourself noticed by senior management because problems are generally visible to them.

- Building your list of accomplishments.

All of these advantages also enhance your professional brand, thus increasing your level of influence within your organization.

PRESENTATION EXCELLENCE

Never underestimate the value of a great speech or presentation. The obvious reason is that people are watching, and in the business world, they are also continually evaluating those they watch.

When you give a presentation at the office, it is usually delivered to:

- Senior management

- Key project stakeholders

- Business peers

- Customers

Your ability to present well to these onlookers:

- Illustrates your business acumen in front of those who control your future.

- Shows your future leadership potential.

- Helps you gain approval and funding for your projects, which enhances your air of success and upward professional mobility.

BE CALM DURING ADVERSITY

Some concepts can be best described with a single quote:

"A man of calm is like a shady tree. People who need shelter come to it."

~Toda Beta, Betelgeuse Incident

You have an advantage in the workplace if you have a reputation for being calm, thinking clearly during times of adversity, and solving difficult issues. People will turn to you when issues arise. This action by others not only increases your reputation, but it provides you with leadership opportunities and maximizes your influence during these turbulent times.

DO EXTRAORDINARY NON-WORK THINGS

Highly respected accomplishments outside the office can raise your level of respect and influence in the workplace because they inspire admiration. We follow those we admire. Have you done any of the following?

- Run marathons or completed ironman triathlons?

- Climbed a high mountain?

- Started a successful charity or local non-profit?

- Any other great things?

If so, don't flaunt it at work—this makes you look like a braggart, but if it's quietly known, people will think of you with respect and be more likely to follow your advice and suggestions.

MENTOR OTHERS

Mentoring subordinates within the organization enhances your skills as a teacher, manager, and leader. It also:

- Builds your reputation as a team player.

- Builds loyalty in those you mentor.

- Makes you more likely to be mentored.

- Builds your "reciprocity bank."

- Positions you for promotion.

- Builds loyal contacts across the company, as those you mentored move to other parts of the company.

Mentoring others also shows your strength of character and your willingness to help others with no expectation of reciprocity. Being viewed this way also enhances your professional brand and importance to the organization.

Building an Influential Professional Brand Worksheet

Brand Building Type	Notes/Actions
Provide execution excellence	
Be proactive	
Use strategic reciprocity	
Provide thought leadership	
Talk about benefits, not features	
Have and show stakeholder empathy	
Take the moral high ground	
Show gratitude	
Illustrate organizational awareness	
Illustrate your passion and conviction	
Be a problem solver	

Building an Influential Professional Brand Worksheet

Brand Building Type	Notes/Actions
Demonstrate presentation excellence	
Be calm during adversity	
Do extraordinary non-work things	
Mentor others	

INFLUENCE POWER RATING (IPR)

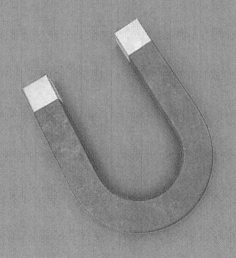

INFLUENCE POWER RATING (IPR)

Influence Power Rating (IPR) calculation brings together two key influence-related concepts. The first concept helps you identify and build your ability to impress, interact with, and gain the respect of others. The second concept is designed to provide an understanding of your ability to influence a predefined person or group on a specific topic at a specific moment.

Your IPR is a calculation based on seventy-four personal and business-related attributes and their effect on your workplace influence, combined with your current situational knowledge of the topic being discussed and your relationship with the person (or people) you are trying to influence.

To understand this calculation, you must first understand the following two key definitions:

Core Influence Characteristics

There are five categories of personal traits that can enhance or detract from your ability to influence others. Understanding and enhancing your personal characteristics increases your overall influential potential. These characteristics are:

- **Personal Attributes:** Who you are as a person

- **Professional Stature:** Your credentials, achievements, and knowledge

- **Interpersonal Skills:** Your ability to communicate with others

- **Business Skills:** Your interaction skills, like negotiation and team building

- **Resources:** Your tangible and intangible assets, like money and connections

Situational Dynamics

In business, all influence is situational. Understanding your relative level of knowledge and control as compared to others is key in assessing your ability to influence them. For example, a business owner has more influence-power over the employees than over the company's customers.

Part 2 of this book describes each item within the IPR calculation and how to use it to your professional advantage. To this end, this section has the following chapters:

- Calculating Your Influence Power Rating (IPR)

- Enhancing Your IPR Personal Attributes

- Enhancing Your IPR Professional Stature

- Enhancing Your IPR Interpersonal Skills

- Enhancing Your IPR Business Skills

- Enhancing Your IPR Resources

- Understanding Workplace Situation Influence

- IPR Attribute Survey Results

While reading through this section and completing the assessments and personal enhancement plans, continually ask yourself the following questions:

1. How can I use each category and element to my professional advantage, influence-related or otherwise?

2. Is my skill, knowledge, and/or use of this category or element hurting my professional or personal growth?

3. How can I improve my skill, knowledge, and/or use of this category or element?

4. How do others view my skill, knowledge, and/or use of this category and element?

In essence, these questions all ask the same thing from different perspectives: "How can this information help me be a better me?"

CALCULATING YOUR INFLUENCE POWER RATING (IPR)

All influence is situational. Understanding your relative level of knowledge and control compared to others is key in assessing your ability to influence them.

~Eric Bloom

This chapter leads you through the IPR calculation. The chapters that follow discuss the Core Influence Characteristics attributes and situational influence definitions in detail.

Calculating your IPR has the following distinct, but related, parts:

- Analyzing Your Core Influence Characteristics (15 minutes)

- Creating a Personal Improvement Plan (optional) (15 minutes)

- Calculating Your Core Influence Characteristics Score (5 minutes)

- Calculating Your Situation Influence (5 minutes each time calculated)

- Combining Steps #3 and #4 to Calculate Your IPR (5 minutes each time calculated)

BACKGROUND

The Influence Power Rating (IPR) will help you assess your ability to influence others. Two components are needed to calculate your IPR.

1. Core Influence Characteristics: Listed below.

2. Situational Influence: The situational dynamics of each interpersonal encounter.

Here is the IPR formula:

$$\left(\underset{1-5}{\underset{\text{Attributes}}{\text{Personal}}} + \underset{1-5}{\underset{\text{Stature}}{\text{Professional}}} + \underset{1-5}{\underset{\text{Skills}}{\text{Interpersonal}}} + \underset{1-5}{\underset{\text{Skills}}{\text{Business}}} + \underset{1-5}{\text{Resources}}\right) \times \underset{0-2}{\underset{\text{Knowledge}}{\text{Situational}}} \times \underset{0-2}{\underset{\text{Audience}}{\text{Situational}}} = \textbf{IPR}$$

Core Influence Characteristics   Situational Influence

This assessment addresses only your Core Influence Characteristics. It will help you understand, measure, and enhance the following personal traits:

- **Personal Attributes:** Who you are as a person

- **Professional Stature:** Your credentials, achievements, and knowledge

- **Interpersonal Skills:** Your communication skills

- **Business Skills:** Your interaction skills, like negotiation and team building

- **Resources:** Your tangible and intangible assets, like money and connections

STEP 1: ANALYZING YOUR CORE INFLUENCE CHARACTERISTICS

Rate yourself from 1–5 on each characteristic using the following criteria:

5 = Strong: A strength of yours personally and professionally

4 = Above average: You feel you are better than most, but have room to improve

3 = Average: You are comfortable with your ability, but not considered an asset

2 = Somewhat weak: A task is difficult but doable with effort and concentration

1 = Weak: Not really in your skill set

Place the number in the Current Ability column after each characteristic.

Core Influence Characteristics Assessment

	Current Ability 1 - 5	Wish to Improve 1 - 5	Priority to Improve 1 - 5	Improvement Order (Wish x Priority)
PERSONAL ATTRIBUTES: INTERNAL				
Builds a reputation of trust and respect				
Confident				
Trustworthy				
Respectful and humble				
Optimistic				
Open-minded				
Empathetic				
Calm				
Transparent				
Humorous				
Authentic				
Courageous				
Creates reputation as a change-agent				
Vision				
Motivation				
Proactive				
Opportunistic				
Creative				
Helps you get the job done				
Commitment				
Flexibility				
Determination				
Accountability				

Core Influence Characteristics Assessment

	Current Ability 1 - 5	Wish to Improve 1 - 5	Priority to Improve 1 - 5	Improvement Order (Wish x Priority)
PERSONAL ATTRIBUTES: EXTERNAL				
Your social connections				
Delegated authority (authority given to you by a person, company, or municipality)				
Friends, allies, and adversaries				
Academic, media, political, and industry contacts				
Your social activities				
Providing thought leadership				
Being an information gateway				
Industry and association activism				
Your actions				
Follow-through				
Showing you care				
Using proper body language				
Leading by example				
Sum of above Current Ability Scores				
Number of Personal Internal Attributes	30			
Number of Personal Internal Attributes				

Core Influence Characteristics Assessment

	Current Ability 1 - 5	Wish to Improve 1 - 5	Priority to Improve 1 - 5	Improvement Order (Wish x Priority)
PROFESSIONAL STATURE				
Your credentials				
College degrees				
Professional certifications				
Profession type				
Job title				
Your credentials				
Awards				
Major accomplishments				
Your knowledge				
Professional experience				
Personal experience				
Learned skills				
Learned information				
Sum of above Current Ability Scores				
Number of Personal Internal Attributes	10			
Category score (Sum/Number of attributes)				

Core Influence Characteristics Assessment

	Current Ability 1 - 5	Wish to Improve 1 - 5	Priority to Improve 1 - 5	Improvement Order (Wish x Priority)
INTERPERSONAL SKILLS				
Builds understanding and empathy				
Emotional intelligence				
Body language				
Enhances fact-finding and builds rapport				
Asking quality questions				
Active listening				
Reduces stress, enhances productivity, facilitates teamwork, and lowers attrition				
Conflict resolution				
Difficult conversations				
Enhances visibility and upward mobility				
Public speaking				
Business acumen				
Facilitation				
Written communication				
Sum of above Current Ability Scores				
Number of Personal Internal Attributes	10			
Category score (Sum/Number of attributes)				

Core Influence Characteristics Assessment

	Current Ability 1 - 5	Wish to Improve 1 - 5	Priority to Improve 1 - 5	Improvement Order (Wish x Priority)
BUSINESS SKILLS				
Helps build your team				
Team building				
Running meetings				
Building diversity				
Vendor management				
Increases productivity and effectiveness				
Consultative approach				
Negotiation				
Tactical influence				
Strategic planning				
Goal setting				
Time management				
Builds loyalty in your team toward you				
Interviewing/Hiring				
Mentoring				
Staff reviews				
Sum of above Current Ability Scores				
Number of Personal Internal Attributes	13			
Category Score (Sum/Number of Attributes)				

Core Influence Characteristics Assessment

	Current Ability 1 - 5	Wish to Improve 1 - 5	Priority to Improve 1 - 5	Improvement Order (Wish x Priority)
RESOURCES				
Money				
Equipment				
Location				
Documentation				
Business process				
Software				
Intellectual property				
Organizational access				
Physical access				
Personal connections				
Relevant information				
Sum of above Current Ability Scores				
Number of Personal Internal Attributes	11			
Category Score (Sum/Number of Attributes)				

STEP 2: CREATING A PERSONAL IMPROVEMENT PLAN (OPTIONAL)

Creating a Personal Improvement Plan is important for your professional growth, but not part of the IPR calculation.

Step 1: To the right of the "Current Ability" column are three additional columns. Complete them as follows:

- **Wish to Improve:** How important to me is improving this characteristic?

  1 = I don't really care.

  2 = It would be nice, but is not required.

  3 = It would have some value to me if easy to attain.

  4 = Improvement would be beneficial to me professionally and/or personally.

  5 = Improvement would be of great value to me professionally and/or personally.

- **Priority to Improve:** Assign a priority to improving this characteristic based on business need

  1 = No need. If I pick it up along the way, great. If not, that is okay too.

  2 = If the opportunity presents itself, I'll read about it or take a class.

  3 = I should definitely look into this at a later time.

  4 = I should work on it this year.

  5 = I should work on this now.

- **Improvement Order: (Wish x Priority) = Improvement Order.** This calculation indicates where you should spend your energy to improve your overall Core Influence Characteristics.

Step 2: Build your self-improvement plan prioritized on the values in the "Improvement Order" column from highest to lowest value.

STEP 3: CALCULATING YOUR CORE INFLUENCE CHARACTERISTICS SCORE

With the Core Influence Characteristics assessment completed (Part 1), you can calculate your Core Influence Characteristics total score. This score is calculated by adding the average score of the five characteristic categories using the following steps:

Step 1: At the bottom of each category, you will see the following rows:

Instructions:

Sum of above Current Ability Scores		Add Current Ability Column values
Number of Personal Internal Attributes	10	The number of attributes in section
Category Score (Sum/Number of Attributes)		Average score

Calculate the "Category score" for each of the categories.

Step 2: Calculate your total score: Add all of your Category score values. This will generate a total score between 5 and 25.

Personal Attributes: _____

Professional Stature: _____

Interpersonal Skills: _____

Business Skills: _____

Resources: _____

TOTAL SCORE: _____

In addition to being used within the IPR calculation, this total score can be used to help you assess your overall professional growth. Over time, as your ability and competency in the Core Influence Characteristics attributes increase, so will your total score.

STEP 4: CALCULATING YOUR SITUATIONAL INFLUENCE

As a reminder, situational influence is the final part of the IPR calculation:

$$\left(\underset{1-5}{\underset{\text{Attributes}}{\text{Personal}}} + \underset{1-5}{\underset{\text{Stature}}{\text{Professional}}} + \underset{1-5}{\underset{\text{Skills}}{\text{Interpersonal}}} + \underset{1-5}{\underset{\text{Skills}}{\text{Business}}} + \underset{1-5}{\text{Resources}}\right) \times \underset{0-2}{\underset{\text{Knowledge}}{\text{Situational}}} \times \underset{0-2}{\underset{\text{Audience}}{\text{Situational}}} = \text{IPR}$$

Core Influence Characteristics | Situational Influence

Now that your Core Influence Characteristics total score is calculated (Step #3), use this total score each time you want to calculate your IPR.

To do so, you must first understand the concept of "Situational Influence":

> **All influence is situational. Understanding your relative level of knowledge and controls compared to others is key in assessing your ability to influence them.**

This definition means that your IPR continually changes depending upon who you are trying to influence. To calculate this value, perform the following steps:

Step 1: Rate yourself from 0–2 based on your Situational Knowledge of the topic being discussed using the following criteria:

- **2 = Strong:** You have a deep understanding of the topic through education, experience, or personal interest compared with those you are trying to influence.

- **1 = Average:** You have a general level of knowledge, but you do not consider yourself an expert compared with those you are trying to influence.

- **0 = Weak:** You have casual or no knowledge on the topic. It is not within your knowledge base compared with those you are trying to influence.

Step 2: Choose the Situational Audience type that best fits your audience and rate yourself on a value of 0–2:

Organizational: This is an audience (individual or group) with a hierarchical structure (such as your boss, parent, or teacher, or when you are the boss, parent, or teacher), causing a formal reporting relationship.

2 = Senior: You are professionally, socially, or organizationally at a higher level than those you are trying to influence.

1 = Peer: You are of equal status professionally, socially, or organizationally with those you are trying to influence.

0 = Junior: You are at a lower status professionally, socially, or organizationally than those you are trying to influence.

Social: There is no formal organizational structure; for example, talking to friends or speaking at a public forum.

2 = Interested: They are very interested in hearing your point-of-view, information, and/or opinion on the subject being discussed.

1 = Neutral: They are casual observers with no vested interest and/or strong opinion on the topic.

0 = Reluctant: They have a difference of opinion on the topic, do not like you personally, and/or disagree with what you are trying to do.

STEP 5: COMBINING STEPS #3 AND #4 TO CALCULATE YOUR IPR

Calculate your score, as the formula illustrates, using the following reduced formula:

$$\text{Core Influence Characteristics} \times \text{Situational Knowledge} \times \text{Situational Audience} = \textbf{IPR}$$

For example, if your calculated values are 19, 2, and 1 respectively, calculate your IPR score as follows:

19 x 2 x 1 = 38

In this second example, let's assume you are known as a thought leader and speaking to a group interested in you and your topic. In this case, your Situational Audience rating = 2: Interested. In this scenario, calculate your IPR as follows:

19 x 2 x 2 = 76

Using this last example, again assume you are a thought leader, but in this case, you will speak on a topic outside your core knowledge. You still have a score of 19 on your Core Influence Characteristics. The audience still loves you, so you still receive a 2 on your Situational Audience rating. However, you know very little about the topic. In this example, your Situation Knowledge rating = 0. Let's see what happens to your IPR.

19 x 2 x 0 = 0

This zero rating means you may want to proceed with caution or decline the offer to speak. If you proceed with the presentation, it could hurt your reputation as a thought leader.

This last (somewhat obvious) example is one of the ways to use IPR to your advantage.

CLOSING THOUGHT

Remember, while your Core Influence Characteristics are somewhat constant but can increase over time, your Situational Influence value must be reassessed with each interpersonal interaction. Therefore, your IPR must also be recalculated on an ongoing basis.

This recalculation will help you be properly prepared for each important workplace interaction, thus enhancing your potential for success and future career advancement.

Good luck using IPR. The chapters that follow will discuss the details of the attributes discussed in this chapter.

ENHANCING YOUR IPR PERSONAL ATTRIBUTES

A leader with great vision but no ability to follow through is like a meal that's all sizzle and no steak.

~Eric Bloom

CATEGORY DESCRIPTION AND STRATEGIC IMPORTANCE

Your personal attributes describe who you are from two perspectives: internal and external. The internal attributes are related to your inner voice, ethics, motivation, veracity, and other similar traits. The external attributes are related to who you know, what you do, and how you act.

These internal and external attributes are related—who you are on the inside affects how you act on the outside—but, from a professional branding and influence perspective, it is more about how you are externally perceived than how you feel internally. In essence, your professional brand and ability to influence others is based on how they perceive you. Remember, their perception of you is their reality.

ELEMENTS THAT BUILD A REPUTATION OF TRUST AND RESPECT

Confidence

- **Definition:** A belief that you can do something well/succeed.

- **Importance:** Your level of internal confidence allows you to speak with conviction and act with purpose. When you inspire others to feel this internal strength and conviction, they will want to follow you. Being humble is also an important attribute.

- **Key Question:** Do those you are trying to influence feel your internal level of confidence? If you are humble, is it hiding your inner strength and belief in yourself?

Trustworthy

- **Definition:** Deserving of trust as observed through actions or deeds.

- **Importance:** Those who do not trust you will not follow you because they are unsure of your true agenda. Also, they will continue to watch their backs in fear that you may turn on them or take advantage of their good nature.

- **Key Question:** When you make a statement to a peer, your staff, your manager, or your clients/customers, do they believe you? Why or why not?

Respectful

- **Definition:** Treating others with courtesy and showing you value their thoughts and opinions.

- **Importance:** Respecting others' opinions, advice, and issues helps build loyalty toward you. This has the benefit of making you more approachable. People will want to approach you with ideas, ask for your assistance, or meet you. This personal connection makes it easier for you to influence them when needed.

- **Key Question:** What did you say and how did you act the last time someone who had nothing you needed asked you a question, asked for your advice, or requested your assistance?

Humble

- **Definition:** Being confident, without excess pride and being willing to listen to others.

- **Importance:** Being humble makes you more approachable and likeable, enhancing your ability to influence others. Being humble is not a sign of weakness; being humble is a sign of confidence, competence, and strength.

- **Key Question:** Do the words you use when describing yourself at a social function sound boastful or factual? Are you overly humble in a way that may hurt your professional growth?

Optimistic

- **Definition:** Having confidence about the future and in the successful completion of important tasks.

- **Importance:** Optimism is a key ingredient in influencing others because it illustrates your belief in success, and everyone wants to be on a winning team.

- **Key Question:** What does the voice in your head say during times of change or adversity? More importantly, from a professional branding perspective, what do other people think the voice in your head is saying?

Open-Minded

- **Definition:** A willingness to listen to others' opinions and suggestions.

- **Importance:** Being open to other points of view allows you to enhance the quality of your vision, the effectiveness of your tactics, and the success of your change management. From an influence perspective, remember, "People who are not part of the solution often become part of the problem."

- **Key Question:** When you have made up your mind, if relevant and important information comes to light, are you willing to reconsider your decision?

Empathetic

- **Definition:** An ability to understand the feelings of others and think about things from their perspective.

- **Importance:** Being able to understand the perspective of others has two primary advantages. First, it provides you the insights to treat them as they would like to be treated. Second, by understanding people's perspectives, motivations, and needs, it's easier to influence them toward required business goals and objectives.

- **Key Question:** Do you spend the time and effort needed to gain an understanding of those you work with? Do you consider the feelings and motivations of others when trying to influence them?

Calm

- **Definition:** Keeping your emotions under control during times of anger, stress, and other business or personal challenges.

- **Importance:** Being calm during challenging times allows you to think more clearly and make better decisions. Also, a person who is calm in the face of challenges is respected by those around them, providing the opportunity for greater influence.

- **Key Question:** How do you act in the face of work challenges? Are you a calming influence on your group when tough decisions need to be made, or are you following others because of their calming effect and ability to take charge when needed?

Transparent

- **Definition:** Being perceived as honest and open and not holding secret business or personal agendas.

- **Importance:** If people think you are honest and open in regard to your business decisions, you have a greater ability to influence people because they believe they can understand things from your perspective.

- **Key Question:** Do those you work with consider you to be open and honest regarding your feelings, decision-making processes, and actions?

Humorous

- **Definition:** Having the ability to be lighthearted and fun at appropriate times.

- **Importance:** If you are fun to be with, people will like you more. Being liked can be used as a key component of influence. Additionally, when humor is used properly, it can make a difficult topic easier to discuss, thus providing a greater ability to inject your point of view.

- **Key Question:** Do you have the ability to appropriately bring humor into the workplace? If yes, how can you use it to your advantage?

Authentic

- **Definition:** Allowing your true personality to be seen by others in the workplace.

- **Importance:** If you are true to yourself by acting as you are, people feel it, and as a result, they will be more likely to trust you. If people think you are not acting authentically and have some type of hidden agenda, they will have their guard up at all times when speaking with you, and they will try to avoid you when possible.

- **Key Question:** Are you authentic at work, or are you trying to act like something you are not?

Courageous

- **Definition:** Having the willingness to make difficult business decisions, take on an appropriate level of calculated risk to meet an important objective, and show a willingness to stand up for your values and ethics.

- **Importance:** People see courage as a virtue. If you are thought of as being courageous in challenging times, you'll be the one they want to follow when times get tough.

- **Key Question:** Are you viewed in the workplace as being courageous? If yes, how can you use this reputation as the person to follow in times of calm and status quo?

ELEMENTS THAT CREATE REPUTATION AS A CHANGE AGENT

Vision

- **Definition:** Ability to define an organization's future direction.

- **Importance:** Vision provides the context for what needs to be done and how you will interact with the people you want to influence. Your vision provides direction and a picture of what you want to achieve.

- **Key Question:** Think quick—what is your vision for your current project, department, or career? If you cannot clearly state it for yourself, you will not be able to articulate it quickly to others when asked.

Motivation

- **Definition:** An internal willingness and drive to act.

- **Importance:** Internal motivation is what causes you to act. If you are not internally motivated to produce a specific outcome, you cannot (or will not) influence others to move toward your defined goal.

- **Key Question:** Are you internally motivated? Why or why not? More importantly, from an influence perspective, do people think you are self-motivated based upon your actions and attitude? Why or why not?

Proactive

- **Definition:** Initiating an action, activity, or task rather than waiting for instruction or something to happen.

- **Importance:** You are proactive when you are the driving force trying to influence others. When you are influenced by others, you are reactive.

- **Key Question:** Do you have the internal drive to initiate tasks that you know should be done, or do you wait for instructions from others?

Opportunistic

- **Definition:** Able to identify and exploit potential opportunities as they arise, without the benefit of a previously defined plan.

- **Importance:** Change is an inevitable part of business. If you are opportunistic, you take advantage of changing business circumstances.

- **Key Question:** Do you view professional risk (or change) as a danger or an opportunity?

Creative

- **Definition:** The ability to think of innovative ideas to solve business issues and identify potential business opportunities.

- **Importance:** If you have a reputation for out-of-the-box thinking, correctly assessing industry trends, and/or finding new potential revenue streams, people will seek out and follow your advice.

- **Key Question:** How can you enhance and illustrate your creative abilities in the workplace?

ELEMENTS THAT HELP GET THE JOB DONE

Commitment:

- **Definition:** Showing dedication to a company, project, or cause.

- **Importance**: Commitment to a company, project, or cause provides multiple influence-related benefits, including opportunities to be proactive and gain the support of those looking for a cause and/or a leader. Build your resume by working on and completing self-directed tasks. Build your reputation as someone who follows through on their commitments.

- **Key Question:** What is the likelihood that you will complete a task or project you start?

Flexibility

- **Definition:** Willingness to change or compromise based on new data, opinions, or experiences.

- **Importance:** If you are flexible, you are able to accept change, and you are willing to change your tactics if a better idea comes along. From an influence perspective, your flexibility shows those you are trying to influence that you are willing to consider another point of view, make adjustments for the good of the project, and be a role model. As a role model, you show others that they should also be flexible and follow your suggested direction.

- **Key Question:** How easy or hard is it for you to accept change? Why or why not?

Determination

- **Definition:** Purposefulness and tenacity in completing tasks and activities.

- **Importance:** Determination illustrates your ability to overcome obstacles for the good of the project. This builds others' respect for you because you are not seen as a quitter. From an influence perspective, when people see you are personally committed to reaching a goal, they want to help. This help is the result of you influencing them to act on your behalf.

- **Key Question:** When you encounter an obstacle to achieving an important business objective, are you more likely to work harder to get through it or to back off and move on to other activities?

Accountability

- **Definition:** A willingness to act and take responsibility for your actions, accepting the results, good or bad.

- **Importance:** Accountability is a combination of demonstrating integrity, being proactive, being willing to admit your mistakes, and accepting how you are judged on your actions. From an influence perspective, people appreciate the personal toughness and leadership personal accountability illustrates. As a result, they will respect and admire you and, therefore, be more willing to follow you.

- **Key Question:** Can you think of a time when a project did not go well? Did you blame others or admit your errors?

YOUR SOCIAL CONNECTIONS

Delegated authority

- **Definition:** Having power based on the authority of another person or organization. For example, a police officer has delegated authority from the governing municipality.

- **Importance:** Delegated authority allows you to act based on others' authority. Within a business context, gaining the support of a senior executive allows you to influence others by using the executive's internal clout, rather than having to rely on your own. In essence, your level of internal influence is elevated to that of your executive sponsor.

- **Key Question:** Is there a higher authority associated with your task, goal, or cause whose allegiance could enhance your authority and ability to influence others?

Friends, allies, and adversaries

- **Definition:** Connections for and against you that you can draw upon or avoid as needed. Sometimes having an enemy can be an advantage—when "the enemy of my enemy is my friend," it means you are aligned with another influential colleague/community member against a common foe.

- **Importance:** Very often in business, you hear the comment that it's not what you know, it's who you know that is important. If you are thought to be very well connected, you can influence others because they hope to use your connections to their advantage, fear you may use your connections against them, and/or believe your objective/vision/project will be successful.

- **Key Question:** Do you have any acquaintances who could enhance your professional brand, bargaining power, or influence if you became more closely aligned?

Academic, media, political, and industry contacts

- **Definition:** Your level of industry activism, your reputation, and your contacts outside your company.

- **Importance:** From an influence perspective, connections to academia show culture and knowledge, to the media show fame, to politicians show power, and to industry show thought leadership. The reality may be different, but to those you are trying to influence, perception is reality.

- **Key Question:** How can you use your academic, media, political, and industry contacts to your advantage?

Your social activities

- **Definition:** Providing thought leadership—business and/or technical vision, inspiration, knowledge, and/or insight to those you want to influence.

- **Importance:** From an influence perspective, teaching others builds loyalty, provides you with a platform of influence, and illustrates your ability and willingness to help others. These characteristics help raise your clout among your peers and others, making it easier to influence them.

- **Key Question:** Is there a way to share your knowledge and insight with others in a helpful way?

Being an information gateway

- **Definition:** Being seen as a person who connects people with people and distributes information (white papers, survey data, research findings, industry event announcements, etc.—not gossip) to those who may be interested.

- **Importance:** From an influence perspective, being an information gateway has two major advantages. First, it keeps you a top-of-mind priority for those you are helping. Second, all these people will feel they owe you a favor. This is known as reciprocity.

- **Key Question:** What information do you receive on an ongoing basis that you could easily and appropriately forward to others just to be nice?

Industry and association activism

- **Definition:** Involvement in industry conferences, associations, and/or user groups, writing for professional publications, or providing input into industry standards and best practices.

- **Importance:** This type of activism has many influence-related advantages, including expanding your professional contacts, staying up-to-date on industry trends, and being viewed by your peers as a thought leader.

- **Key Question:** What is your current level of industry activism? Would it be of professional value to increase your level of industry activism? If yes, what could you do?

YOUR ACTIONS

Following through

- **Definition:** Keeping your promises, completing agreed-upon tasks, keeping your commitments, and working diligently toward your vision and objectives.

- **Importance:** Having a clear vision is a key competent in influencing people initially, but to keep them engaged and following your direction, you must continue to hold up your part of the deal.

- **Key Question:** When you make a commitment or promise something, do others believe you will deliver? Why or why not?

Showing you care

- **Definition:** A willingness to have empathy for others and demonstrate empathy in your conversations and actions.

- **Importance:** There is an old expression, "People don't care what you know until they know that you care."

- **Key Question:** When was the last time you showed a friend or business colleague you care about one of their issues? What did you say, and what did you do?

Using proper body language

- **Definition:** Body language can be both structural and observational. When you use body language purposefully, it is structural body language. You use your posture and movements to convey the attitudes you want others to see. Observational body language is when you watch the posture and movements of others to better understand their thoughts, attitudes, and positions.

- **Importance:** Structural body language allows you to portray the image you want others to see and to influence them. Observational body language can help you decide whom to influence and/or if your influence is working.

- **Key Question:** Do you consciously pay attention to your body language and/or the body language of others? Why or why not?

Leading by example

- **Definition:** Influencing people to act based on your actions.

- **Importance:** One of Steve Jobs' most famous quotes is: "Leaders lead by example whether they want to or not." Never underestimate the effect your actions have on others.

- **Key Question:** If the people with whom you work acted like you act, would you respect them and possibly be influenced by them? Why or why not?

Enhancing Your IPR Personal Attributes Worksheet

Personal Attributes	Notes/Actions
Confidence	
Trustworthiness	
Respectfulness	
Humility	
Optimism	
Open-Mindedness	
Empathetic	
Calm	
Transparent	
Humorous	
Authentic	
Courageous	
Elements that create a reputation as a change-agent	
Vision	
Motivation	
Proactiveness	
Opportunistic	
Creative	

Enhancing Your IPR Personal Attributes Worksheet

Personal Attributes	Notes/Actions
Elements that help get the job done	
Commitment	
Flexibility	
Determination	
Accountability	
Your social connections	
Delegated authority	
Friends, allies, and adversaries	
Academic, media, political, and industry contacts	
Your social activities	
Being an information gateway	
Industry and association activism	
Your actions	
Following through	
Showing you care	
Using proper body language	
Leading by example	

ENHANCING YOUR IPR PROFESSIONAL STATURE

Your college degrees can definitely help you find a job, but they won't keep you employed—that requires work, skill, knowledge, and luck.

~Eric Bloom

CATEGORY DESCRIPTION AND STRATEGIC IMPORTANCE

Your professional stature is how you are viewed by others in regard to your credentials, achievements, and overall knowledge. This stature, however, is not constant. It ebbs and flows based on the people with whom you are interacting. This phenomenon is described in Chapter 19: Understanding Workplace Situational Influence. Basically, the level of your stature is viewed differently by different people based on the topic being discussed, the circumstance of the meeting, and the credentials of those with whom you're meeting.

That said, working to enhance your credentials, accomplishments, and knowledge can dramatically enhance your influence. With greater stature and a more powerful peer group, you will have more people below your level of stature who will be easier to influence.

In addition to the influence it provides, don't underestimate the other potential professional advantages of enhancing your credentials, accomplishments, and knowledge.

YOUR CREDENTIALS

The importance of credentials varies greatly from profession to profession. In some professions, specific college degrees and certifications are a regulatory requirement. For example, all lawyers in the United States must attend law school and pass their state's bar exam. As a second example, all doctors must go to medical school and pass the certification exams within their specific medical disciplines. While these types of credentials are in themselves very admirable and impressive, from an influence perspective, their value varies greatly depending on the audience and situation.

At a medical convention of heart surgeons, a heart surgeon is just one of many with the same qualifications. To stand out among this group, a surgeon must be special in some other way, like having attended a prestigious college, practicing at a highly respected hospital, or holding a position of influence within the hospital, such as head of surgery. This surgeon may also be considered a leader among this peer group based on achievements and/or knowledge, which we will discuss later in this chapter.

In other professions, such as project management, no specific college degree or certification is required. However, the Project Management Professional (PMP) certification sponsored by the Project Management Institute (PMI) is very highly regarded and required by many companies hiring project managers and people in related roles. From an influence perspective, having a PMP carries great weight.

Specific types of credentials are described below:

Degrees

- **Definition:** A degree indicates your level of academic achievement, including associate's, bachelor's, master's, and doctorate degrees. It may also include university-sponsored post-master's and post-doctorate designations.

- **Importance:** Has great value from many perspectives.

- **Key Questions:** How can you use your college degrees to their maximum value? Also, could an additional degree have a dramatic effect on your career and/or influence?

Certifications

- **Definition:** There are many types of certifications. Generally speaking, a certification requires an exam and is associated with a specific skill or product. For example, a certification in IT management would include the general skills needed to lead technical professionals. Alternately, a certification in Microsoft Windows 10 shows competency on that particular operating system.

- **Importance:** The value is profession-specific. From an influence perspective, the benefit is questionable unless the certificate is highly regarded within the profession of those who are certified. Outside this professional area these certifications, generally, carry little influence value because people don't see the value beyond a particular skill.

- **Key Questions:** How can you maximize the value of your current certifications? Are there other certifications within your profession that would add value to your career or influence?

Profession type

- **Definition:** This is your profession, for example, human resources, finance, legal, sales, etc.

- **Importance:** Within a specific organization, some professions are more highly regarded than others. For example, in financial services, the portfolio managers and research analysts run the show and have virtually all the influence within the firm. IT professionals within these financial services firms may be respected, but they have no real influence. Alternatively, if this same IT professional changes jobs and begins work at a software company in product engineering, they will be highly respected and have an influential role within the company because they are creating the products the company sells.

- **Key Questions:** Do you work at a company where your job type is highly valued, and thus, influential within your firm? If your job type is not highly valued and respected within your company, are there other benefits, such as being highly compensated, that make staying worthwhile?

Job title

- **Definition:** This is...well, your job title. I don't know how else to describe it.

- **Importance:** From an influence perspective, your job title carries significant weight if your level of responsibility matches the title. For example, being the vice president of marketing in a three-person company is very different from having the same title in a $100 million company. On the downside, having major responsibility and a poor job title can hurt your influence. For example, being the IT security manager would not be as marketable as being the "Chief Information Security Officer."

- **Key Questions:** Does your job title accurately represent the work you do and your level of responsibility?

YOUR ACHIEVEMENTS

Your achievements are a combination of awards and major accomplishments. These have the potential to dramatically and quickly enhance your reputation, professional stature, and, of course, your level of influence.

Awards

- **Definition:** These are company, professional, industry, and non-business awards that have a positive effect on you personally or professionally. Company awards may include Employee of the Year or Top Salesperson. Professional awards are generally related to a professional association, for example, the National Speakers Association has the Speaker Hall of Fame. Entertainment industry-related awards include the Emmy, Oscar, etc. Personal awards are not work- or career-oriented, but illustrate your great character, charitable nature, civic contribution, etc.

- **Importance:** These awards illustrate your abilities, character, or success recognized by others. These types of awards are of great value to you professionally, even if they are not for professionally-oriented accomplishments. The value is not in saying how good you are; it is in other people saying how good you are. This single distinction gives these awards weight and credibility.

- **Key Questions:** What awards have you received that would be worthwhile to publicize quietly (or not so quietly)? Are there any awards that you respect and aspire to receive? If yes, what steps can you take to increase your chances of receiving them?

Major accomplishments

- **Definition:** These are noteworthy achievements performed both inside and outside the workplace. In the workplace, this could be a scientific discovery, writing a bestselling book, or some other hard-to-achieve accomplishment. Outside the office, it could be climbing Mount Kilimanjaro, being an Olympic athlete, or another personal endeavor that would bring the admiration of others.

- **Importance:** Your accomplishments, whether they be inside or outside the workplace, say something about you as a person. As a result, they can elevate people's opinions and respect for you as a person. This, in turn, enhances your ability to influence them.

- **Key Questions:** Do you have any major accomplishments that would impress your coworkers and raise your stature and influence in the workplace?

YOUR KNOWLEDGE

Your knowledge is a combination of your professional experience, technical and business skills, and your knowledge of business-related topics. Note that having this knowledge is not enough. Others must believe you have this knowledge and that you are both willing to share it with others and use it for the company's benefit.

Experience

- **Definition:** Your professional experience related to your current job. This may also include personal experiences and wisdom gained through age if it is relevant to your work-related decision making.

- **Importance:** This is of great importance only if your past experiences have allowed you to learn from your mistakes, widened your perspective, and enhanced your professional craft.

- **Key Questions:** How can you take advantage of your past professional and personal experience? How can you share these experiences with others to enhance your professional stature and office influence?

Learned skills

- **Definition:** Learned skills are skills of value to your current job. Other skills, such as learning to play piano as a child or having been a COBOL programmer in the 1980s, while of personal interest, are only of value in the workplace if they provide some type of professional value.

- **Importance:** Your learned skills are the basis for your professional craft. From an influence perspective, your level of influence will be heavily based on your skills relative to the skills of those whom you are trying to influence.

- **Key Questions:** Do you have any previously acquired skills you are not taking advantage of in your current role that could be used to your advantage?

Learned information

- **Definition:** Learned information is the information you have acquired throughout your life, both professional and personal.

- **Importance:** The more relevant to your current role, the higher the value. This learned information could also include knowledge that is of value building personal relationships with coworkers. For example, if you and your boss both have a strong interest in sports trivia, this common bond could increase your friendship, thus increasing your influence with both your boss and your peers.

- **Key Questions:** Are there any opportunities for self-study that could enhance your current job performance and/or increase your potential chance of promotion? Do you have any additional job or non-job-related knowledge that could potentially be used to your advantage in the workplace?

Enhancing Your IPR Professional Stature Worksheet

Professional Stature Attributes	Notes/Actions
Your credentials	
Degrees	
Certifications	
Profession type	
Job title	
Your achievements	
Awards	
Major accomplishments	
Your knowledge	
Experience	
Learned skills	
Learned information	

ENHANCING YOUR IPR INTERPERSONAL SKILLS

Enhancing your ability to communicate effectively with others is neither an event nor a destination. It's a journey of life-long learning, practice, and experience.

~Eric Bloom

The ability to connect with others at a personal and professional level is key to your ability to influence them. This connection may be one-to-one or one-to-many, depending on your organizational level, job role, and/or influence goal. A potential new hire trying to influence the hiring manager is an example of a one-to-one connection. An example of a one-to-many connection is a senior executive attempting to influence the entire team by delivering a single speech at an all-hands meeting.

While these two interactions seemingly require very different interpersonal communication skills, they have more in common than meets the eye. The major difference is the delivery mechanism—conversation versus presentation.

Whether one-to-one or one-to-many, both communication types require a variety of common skills that we take for granted as part of human nature:

Emotional Intelligence: Allows you to understand and manage yourself and exhibit empathy and an understanding of others.

Body language: Puts you in control of presenting yourself in the best possible light and allows you to analyze and assess others' attitudes.

Questioning and Listening: Asking purposeful questions combined with active listening skills illustrates business acumen, facilitates understanding, and builds relationships.

Conflict: Combination of conflict avoidance, conflict resolution, and the ability to navigate difficult conversations effectively allows you to:

> **Reduce stress:** Stress is reduced because there will be less tension within the group.

> **Facilitate teamwork:** When internal department conflicts are resolved, the team mindset can grow because there is less positioning and bickering within the group.

Enhance productivity: Productivity is enhanced when people spend less mental energy developing strategies to protect themselves from their teammates and more time thinking about how to help the organization meet its goals and objectives.

Increase job satisfaction: When department stress is reduced, teamwork is felt by all, productivity is enhanced, and work is more satisfying and enjoyable. This enhanced environment increases job satisfaction because people are happy to be there.

Lower attrition: If people are happy at work, feel part of a team, are productive, and have job satisfaction, they are less likely to look for employment elsewhere.

Lastly, the ability to communicate, both verbally and in writing, and to connect one-to-one and one-to-many, can dramatically enhance your visibility and upward mobility. Email and other written documents are long-lasting artifacts of your knowledge, skills, business acumen, and abilities. Your verbal one-on-one communication builds personal relationships, trust, and respect. One-to-many communication enhances your professional reputation, influences decision-makers, and improves your professional brand.

BUILDING YOUR UNDERSTANDING AND EMPATHY

Emotional intelligence

- **Definition:** Emotional intelligence (EQ) has two key aspects. First, it is the ability to understand yourself in a way that allows you to properly manage your actions and emotions. Second, it is the ability to understand others using empathy and organizational awareness with the goal of influencing them to aid in obtaining your objectives.

- **Importance:** EQ is of great importance. If you take away only one concept from this book regarding influencing others, it should be about emotional intelligence.

- **Key Questions:** How can you use EQ to influence others? How can you use EQ to grow as a person and a professional?

Body language

- **Definition:** Body language is nonverbal communication using unconscious or conscious body movement, posture, and gestures.

- **Importance:** The importance of body language is twofold. First, people judge your sincerity, strength, confidence, competency, and other attributes based on their interpretation of your body language. Second, you can gain insight into how others feel about you by understanding their body language.

- **Key Questions:** How do people interpret your body language, and is it to your benefit or detriment? Do you understand enough about body language to use it to your advantage? If not, what is the best way to expand your knowledge?

ENHANCING YOUR FACT-FINDING ABILITY

Asking purposeful questions

- **Definition:** Purposeful questions are questions specifically asked with the intent of causing a desired outcome. For example, a leading question, like, "Do you have any additional questions before we sign the contract?" is really a polite way of saying, "Sign the contract."

- **Importance:** When trying to influence others, asking a good question is often more effective than making a statement. A question makes people come to their own conclusion, which allows them to feel more in control of the situation.

- **Key Question:** How can you rephrase statements as questions that influence others to follow your desired direction?

Active listening

- **Definition:** Active listening is a technique of listening to others in a way that maximizes understanding between the speaker and listener while simultaneously, through comments and/or body language, shows the speaker that the listener is paying attention.

- **Importance:** The better you can understand a person's perspective on a topic, the easier it is to influence them in a way that is consistent and/or related to their point of view.

- **Key Questions:** Have you ever studied active listening? If yes, how can you strategically use it to influence others? If not, do you think it would be worthwhile to invest the time to enhance your listening skills?

REDUCING STRESS, ENHANCING PRODUCTIVITY, FACILITATING TEAMWORK, AND LOWERING ATTRITION

Conflict resolution

- **Definition:** Conflict resolution is turning unhealthy conflict into a workable solution through brainstorming, negotiation, compromise, common goal setting, and other related activities.

- **Importance:** We discussed the importance at length in this chapter's introduction.

- **Key Questions:** What potential conflicts do you anticipate may arise in your office/project that could be avoided with early intervention? What conflicts could you help resolve to enhance your influence within the workplace?

Difficult conversations

- **Definition:** The ability to calmly and effectively talk one-on-one to another person with whom you have a conflict in an effort to make the situation workable and comfortable for both parties.

- **Importance:** Also discussed at length in the chapter's introduction.

- **Key Questions:** Currently, how do you prepare for difficult conversations? Do you have a standard script or process you like to follow? Are you putting off any difficult conversations that would help you meet your business objectives? If yes, why have you delayed?

ENHANCING YOUR VISIBILITY AND UPWARD MOBILITY

Business acumen

- **Definition:** Business acumen is the ability to understand and successfully deal with business challenges and opportunities as they arise through thought leadership, vision, problem solving, and creativity. It also includes the ability to communicate your vision (the big picture) to your team, peers, and organizational leadership.

- **Importance:** Your ability to quickly understand and adapt to a changing business landscape within your company, industry, and the greater economy positions you to influence others because of your insights and your ability to articulate them.

- **Key Questions:** How can you better understand your business environment and turn this newfound knowledge into actionable objectives? Is your level of business acumen helping or hurting your ability to move ahead professionally? Why?

Public speaking

- **Definition:** Delivering a public speech or giving a presentation within your organization.

- **Importance:** Presentations are given to an audience you are trying to influence, impress, secure agreement from, motivate, inform, and/or educate. The ability to present well in front of others is not the goal—it is an important tool needed to meet your business and professional objectives.

- **Key Questions:** Given the above definition, do you feel comfortable, confident, and successful speaking in public? If not, how can you enhance your public speaking skills? If yes, how can you use this tool to your advantage?

Facilitation

- **Definition:** Facilitation, within a business meeting context, is the ability to assume the responsibility of guiding a discussion within the group, without imposing your thoughts or agenda on the discussion. For example, if you are leading a brainstorming discussion, your goal is to get others to step up and accept responsibility while you remain impartial.

- **Importance:** From an influence perspective, this type of facilitation allows you to take a leadership role in a discussion where you have limited personal experience, stature, and/or knowledge.

- **Key Question:** How can your ability to facilitate discussions on topics where you are not the subject-matter expert enhance your professional brand and organizational stature?

Written communication

- **Definition:** Written communication, within this context, is your ability to deliver your message to others via email, status reports, formal documentation, blogs, and other business-related, written artifacts.

- **Importance:** Your ability to write well has three primary business advantages. First, it helps you meet your business objectives by clearly explaining situations and needed results. Second, it allows you to document your success in status-type reports that will be used to assess your job performance. Third, it allows you to influence the reader to follow your recommendations, instructions, and/or requests.

- **Key Questions:** Do you consider yourself a good writer? If yes, how can you use this ability to your advantage to influence others? If not, what can you do in the short term to minimize the adverse effect on your professional brand? In the long term, how can you improve your writing skills to help meet your business goals? Answers might include: by taking a class, doing personal research, finding a writing mentor to review your documents, and of course, practicing. Simple techniques, such as limiting sentences to one idea each, can help make your writing much more readable, and thus, more influential.

Enhancing Your IPR Interpersonal Skills Worksheet

Interpersonal Skills	Notes/Actions
Build your understanding and empathy	
Emotional intelligence	
Body language	
Enhance your fact-finding ability	
Ask purposeful questions	
Listen actively	
Reduce stress, enhance productivity, facilitate teamwork, and lower attrition	
Conflict resolution	
Difficult conversations	
Enhancing your visibility and upward mobility	
Business acumen	
Public speaking	
Facilitation	
Written communication	

ENHANCING YOUR IPR BUSINESS SKILLS

Individual commitment to a group effort—that is what makes a team work, a company work, a society work, a civilization work.

~Vince Lombardi

Business skills are in many ways the culmination of your personal attributes, professional stature, and interpersonal communication. Your personal attributes are trust, respect, confidence, and tenacity. Your professional stature brings credibility. Your interpersonal skills bring an understanding of others, conversational ease, and interpersonal connection. Lastly, your business skills, supercharged by these previously described characteristics, enhance your leadership ability, management competence, business effectiveness, and ability to inspire team loyalty.

BUILDING YOUR TEAM

The attributes in this section produce strong management competency. Managers with the ability to create a culture of teamwork within their departments sow the seeds of productivity, staff job satisfaction, low attrition, and professional growth for their teams and upward mobility for themselves.

Running an effective and efficient meeting should appear easy to participants. The truth is, like most things that look easy, it's much harder than it looks. Doing it well, however, helps you meet your business objectives, enhances your professional brand, and gets people to want to attend your meetings.

Properly building diversity within your team is more than simply complying with diversity as defined in legal and moral terms related to gender and ethnicity. While that is of great importance, it's not enough. Purposefully building diversity of thought and experience gives your team increased creativity, increased problem-solving ability, and a wider variety of skills, knowledge, and professional contacts.

You should also expand your concept of team to include the vendors you hire. Hiring and managing the right vendor is as important as hiring and managing the right employee. The right vendor, depending on its role, can dramatically increase your chance of project success, provide valuable insight needed to solve difficult business challenges, and/or act as a valued extension of your department's resources and capabilities.

Team building

- **Definition:** Your ability as an official or unofficial leader to bring a group together as a cohesive and functional team.

- **Influence importance:** If you build a spirit of teamwork within the group, you will be viewed as a group leader, thus increasing your level of influence within the group. This enhanced level of influence increases the likelihood that the group will take your advice and direction at a future time.

- **Key Questions:** What could you do now to strengthen your group's teamwork, cohesion, and/or success?

Running meetings

- **Definition:** The ability to herd cats…. Sorry. The ability to get strategic or tactical value from a meeting in an orderly and appropriate manner, given the situation, group, content, and objective.

- **Influence Importance:** Running a high-quality meeting has many influence advantages during and after the meeting. During the meeting, you drive the agenda and, by definition, control the room. After the meeting, you can use the meeting's momentum to continue this control at a lesser level.

- **Key Questions:** What do people who attend your meetings say about them? How do you know that's what they say? When thinking about meetings you attend as a participant, what can you learn from how those meetings are run to improve your ability in the future?

Building diversity

- **Definition:** The ability to build a well-rounded team containing the variety of skills, personalities, backgrounds, and experience needed to maximize team creativity and effectiveness.

- **Influence Importance:** Creating well-rounded teams enhances the potential for success. It also illustrates your leadership ability by demonstrating how well you work with an assortment of people with varying skills and backgrounds.

- **Key Questions:** How diverse is your group? Do you feel comfortable working with and/or leading people with diverse backgrounds?

Vendor management

- **Definition:** The ability to identify, evaluate, select, negotiate, hire, manage, and measure vendors.

- **Influence Importance:** Hiring and managing the right vendor is key to your success as a business professional and organizational leader. This ability enhances your organizational influence because strong vendor management reduces project risk, increases the potential of project success, and illustrates strong leadership and decision-making abilities.

- **Key Questions:** What can you do to increase your current vendors' effectiveness? What lessons have you learned regarding managing vendors that could increase your future effectiveness?

INCREASING PRODUCTIVITY AND EFFECTIVENESS

These items drive business. Taking a consultative approach to your work with clients, whether they are internal or external customers, helps maximize the satisfaction of those using the output of your individual efforts and/or department's output.

The ability to negotiate is a core business skill that is advantageous in almost all business situations. If done properly, it saves money, helps you attain needed resources, soothes interpersonal conflict, and helps advance your career.

Tactical influence is using concepts like reciprocity, authority, and liking (Cialdini-based items) to change others' short-term actions and decisions.

Strategic planning provides both professional and influential advantages. Professional advantage comes from being able to define and plan the future. Influential advantage comes from providing vision-type currency (Cohen-Bradford-based item) for those looking for someone or something to follow.

Goal setting is a key business skill and extremely influential because it provides an objective to march toward. If the goal is SMART (specific, measurable, attainable, relevant, and time-bound), it also tightly defines the required result.

Time management is key from both an individual and organizational perspective. The better your individual time management, the more time you will have to perform valued work. Organizationally, the better the time management, the higher the productivity.

Consultative approach

- **Definition:** A consultative approach means treating those you are supporting with respect and understanding. It also means being able to provide thought leadership, being willing to truly listen to your client's needs, and being flawless in executing the required tasks.

- **Influence Importance:** Having a consultative approach provides two influence-enhancing benefits: creative vision and dependability. First, having a reputation of creative vision through thought leadership causes people to seek your advice on solving business challenges and exploiting potential business opportunities. Giving advice allows you to influence business decisions and outcomes. Also, you are building a feeling of obligation (reciprocity) in the people to whom you provide advice. Second, a reputation of being dependable helps make you the go-to person when issues and opportunities arise. When people come to you, rather than you going to them, it increases your influence regarding how things should be done.

- **Key Questions:** Do you have an internal company reputation as a thought leader and/or as being dependable. If yes, how can you use this to your advantage? If not, what can you do to enhance your internal reputation?

Negotiation

- **Definition:** From a business perspective, negotiation is the process of working with others to define the terms of a contract, business deal, conflict resolution, resource allocation, project delivery schedule, or other related items.

- **Influence Importance:** The ability to negotiate well has many positive business benefits, including gaining favorable business terms and getting the internal resources to maximize the potential of a project's success. From an influence perspective, a reputation for negotiating well enhances your professional reputation and causes people to be on your side of a deal or office discussion.

- **Key Questions:** Have you ever studied negotiation? If not, would learning more about how to negotiate enhance your career or personal success? How could you use influence-based techniques to enhance negotiation success?

Strategic planning

- **Definition:** Strategic planning is the process of systematically envisioning a desired future state (strategic thinking), translating this vision into broadly defined goals, and then defining a sequence of steps (project plan) to achieve the overall goal.

- **Influence Importance:** The strategic planning process includes various influence-generating activities, including the creation of a vision (strategic thinking), articulation of the vision (writing and presenting), and project planning. Each of these individually enhances your influential appeal. Combined, they position you as an internal agent of change and a thought leader.

- **Key Questions:** Given your current job role and level of responsibility, how can you be perceived as a person of vision and creativity? What can you do proactively to enhance the internal productivity of your department or company and your own, and how can you use these ideas to enhance your overall influence and potential for career advancement?

Goal setting

- **Definition:** Goal setting is the combination of identifying a needed objective and defining its timeframe, attributes, and how success will be measured.

- **Influence Importance:** Goal setting is a form of actionable vision. Its creation gives people a purpose to accept as their own and move forward toward its completion. The timeframe, attributes, and measurable results allow you to steer peoples' energy in the proper direction toward your objective.

- **Key Questions:** Are you familiar with the term SMART Goals? If yes, are you using them to your professional advantage? If not, learn about them, and then ask yourself how you can use them to your advantage.

Time management

- **Definition:** Time management is the process of prioritizing your time (and/or the time of others) in a way that best helps you meet your goals and objectives.

- **Influence Importance:** Time management is a key component of influence because it:
  - » Gives you the time to influence others.
  - » Allows you to achieve more, which enhances others' respect toward you.
  - » Illustrates that you will not be wasting people's time.
  - » Shows that you are organized and can meet your work deadlines.

- **Key Questions:** How efficiently do you use your time and the time of others? Are there any time-management techniques you could use to enhance your or others' efficiency?

BUILDING LOYALTY IN YOUR TEAM TOWARD YOU

This section's attributes are primarily for those in management/leadership positions who interview and hire new staff, write performance reviews, and mentor staff. Very often, however, many senior individuals are also involved in interviewing and performance reviews. Leaders with the ability to hire the right people, who help their people grow through instruction and mentoring, and who take care to give instructive, factual, and fair performance reviews for their staff, build loyalty in their staff toward them.

This is the case because of the influence that leaders can have on the careers of those working for them. Additionally, if a manager cares about their staff, the staff feels it, appreciates it, and returns it in kind.

Interviewing/Hiring

- **Definition:** The process of bringing new employees into your group.

- **Influence Importance:** The interviewing and hiring process is one of a manager's most important activities. If you hire the right people, it enhances your team's culture, productivity, effectiveness, and overall success. If you hire the wrong people, they become poster children for your poor decision-making ability.

- **Key Questions**: Do you put in the required time and effort to hire good people, or do you view the hiring process as just another management task to be completed?

Mentoring

- **Definition:** Mentoring takes many forms: technical instructor, career coach, professional advocate, protector, resource provider, role model, and, sometimes, life coach.

- **Influence Importance:** The more you mentor your team and others within the company, the wider your scope of influence because mentoring others builds loyalty in them toward you. Then, as time goes on, those you have mentored will move to other parts of the company at different organizational levels. This network can provide you influence well beyond your specific area of responsibility, even beyond your company, as those whom you have mentored seek opportunities in other organizations.

- **Key Questions:** Whom should you be mentoring, inside and outside your team, for their professional advantage and to enhance your current and future level of influence? Do you have a mentor to help you professionally?

Staff reviews

- **Definition:** Writing and delivering employee performance reviews. Such reviews should also include ongoing, informal, impromptu employee feedback throughout the performance period.

- **Influence Importance:** The time you take in providing feedback to your team will be returned in loyalty. Additionally, feedback to staff enhances their performance, which, in turn, enhances team effectiveness. The greater your team's effectiveness, the stronger your personal reputation, and thus, your influence.

- **Key Questions:** Do you take the time to write insightful and thorough performance reviews? Do you provide ongoing feedback to your staff that will help them grow as professionals and enhance their current job performance?

Enhancing Your IPR Business Skills Worksheet

Personal Attribute	Notes/Actions
Building your team	
Team building	
Running meetings	
Building diversity	
Vendor management	
Increasing productivity and effectiveness	
Consultative approach	
Negotiation	
Strategic planning	
Goal setting	
Time management	
Building loyalty in your team toward you	
Interviewing/Hiring	
Mentoring	
Staff reviews	

ENHANCING YOUR IPR RESOURCES

Just because you have the money, doesn't mean you necessarily have the ability to force others to follow your lead. In effect, you can always say no by withholding funds, but you can't always make others say yes.

~Eric Bloom

Of the five core influence characteristics, "Enhancing Your IPR Resources" is the only one not about who you are or what you have done. This influence category is related to what you have. The concept behind this influence type is recognition that office influence can also be heavily swayed by controlling the budget, intellectual property, connections, and other related items. This concept falls under the children's premise that, "It's my ball, so I decide the rules." It may seem that having the money is the main factor within this list. While control of budget dollars certainly is a key factor, each of the other items, particularly control of intellectual property, can play a defining role in who calls the shots.

Money/Budget

- **Definition:** This is the person who controls the project's funding.

- **Importance:** If you are the one with the money, you can say no to the project by not providing the needed cash. However, just because you have the money doesn't mean you necessarily have the ability to force others to follow your lead.

- **Key Question:** From a company and an influence perspective, are you using your budget dollars to their greatest business advantage?

Equipment

- **Definition:** Equipment is physical items, such as computers, servers, trucks, construction equipment, and other objects where whoever controls them has a certain level of power within the group/project.

- **Importance:** The equipment you bring to the table may be of importance or insignificant from an influence perspective. It will depend upon how crucial your equipment is to completing the task and how easily it can be replaced.

- **Key Question:** What is the true value of your equipment in your influence over others? How easily can your equipment be replaced by those you are trying to influence? Can the project be completed without your equipment through alternative means?

Location

- **Definition:** Location is the office, a conference room, a technological medium, or any other venue where the meeting may be held.

- **Importance:** In the workplace, location is generally not a major influence factor, but it may have a subliminal benefit.

- **Key Question:** If location is an important factor to you, how can you orchestrate location selection to your advantage? The sporting equivalent is having home field advantage. In the workplace, this could be as simple as choosing whether to have a meeting in your office or another space.

Documentation

- **Definition:** Documentation is the data and/or access necessary to perform a task. The documents can be physical or electronic.

- **Importance:** The importance of documentation, from an influence perspective, is based on its value to the desired outcome. For example, if there is a treasure hunt and you own the treasure map, you are in a very influential position for as long as the document is needed.

- **Key Question:** How can you maximize the value of your documentation? How can you minimize the need for documentation from other sources to reduce their influence over you?

Business Process

- **Definition:** This refers to your organization's predefined processes that you can use to your advantage in a specific situation. For example, your department may have expertise in a needed methodology, such as Six Sigma or Agile, required to run a project properly. This process expertise gives your department, and you personally, a high level of influence.

- **Importance:** Like others in this category, importance is based upon the specific need for your processes and the potential cost of obtaining them elsewhere.

- **Key Question:** How can you maximize the value of your department's processes to maximize your team's value to your company and its influence over other departments? How can you minimize the need for other business processes to reduce their influence over you?

Software

- **Definition:** This includes any computer applications used within your department that have been purchased, built, or subscribed to.

- **Importance**: The importance of your software from an influence perspective is based on its importance to the project you are trying to influence and how easily and at what cost it can be replicated or replaced.

- **Key Question:** How can you increase the value of your department's software to maximize your team's value and influence? How can you minimize the need for others' software to reduce their influence over you?

Intellectual Property

- **Definition:** Intellectual Property (IP) can include information, processes, techniques, methodologies, data, or other related items. Unlike other characteristics in this category, IP can potentially be copyrighted, patented, trademarked, and/or controlled by the use of non-disclosure agreements. IP of this type cannot be legally copied or used without the owner's consent. In most cases, however, IP is not legally protected—it is simply protected using limited access, computer security, and other process-based methods.

- **Importance:** The influence potential of IP can range from inconsequential to indispensable.

- **Key Question:** Do you have IP within your department that could be used in new and innovative ways that would be of value to your company?

Physical Access

- **Definition:** This refers to having needed authority, security, and permission to use a specific location.

- **Importance:** From an influence perspective, your value and level of influence increases based on the difficulty of gaining access combined with the desire to gain access. For example, if you work in a lab environment and have access to the equipment in a specialized lab, this provides you influence over others who want to use the lab.

- **Key Question:** Do you have access to any physical locations? They could be conference rooms, a local sports team's skybox, or other space that you could better use to your professional advantage when influencing others.

Organizational Access

- **Definition:** Organization access refers to those you have access to who hold important positions within your company. For example, a college intern working in the accounting department will possess far greater internal influence than expected if this intern is the child of the company's CEO's.

- **Importance:** These types of internal connections to senior officials carry two types of influence: passive and active. Passive influence is simply people knowing you have important, high-level connections. Active influence is either initiated through a request to your senior advocate or when your senior advocate performs an action on your behalf without your request, such as facilitating a promotion, saving you from layoffs, or making sure you are assigned to great projects.

- **Key Question:** If you don't currently have a senior-level advocate/connection who can increase your influence and accelerate career advancement, how can you get one?

Personal Connections

- **Definition:** Personal connections are people you know personally, outside of the company, who could provide you with influence inside your company. For example, you have a family member or next-door neighbor who is a senior executive at a company your firm is trying to get as a client.

- **Importance:** The level of internal company influence these people create is based on the combination of your company's need to access them and your comfort and ability to make meaningful connections.

- **Key Question:** Whom do you know outside your workplace who could be of great advantage to you inside your workplace?

Information

- **Definition:** Information here refers to information that has value to others, is not hidden but is largely unknown, and that you have uncovered through research, data analysis, or luck.

- **Importance:** The influence-based value of this type of information hinges on its importance to others. For example, if through data analysis you discover a previously unknown correlation between two factors that can be used by your company to increase sales, it could be of great value to your internal influence and professional growth.

- **Key Question:** Do you know of any important information that, upon deeper consideration, would be of value to others within your company?

The various tangible characteristics listed in this category can be combined to dramatically enhance your and/or your department's influence. For example, the combination of purchased software and internal business processes can be very hard to replicate. If this combination is important to others and hard to replicate, it increases your potential influence because it's easier and less expensive to tap into your group's capabilities than to recreate them or go to the trouble of finding another partner.

Within a corporate environment, these types of assets can be used both for and against you. While you are trying to use your assets to influence others, others are trying to use their assets to gain influence over you. In some workplace situations, this is done subtly, almost invisibly. In other work situations, it's done directly, blatantly, and occasionally, with wrongful intent.

This chapter's goal is twofold: 1) To explain how you can use your available assets for the good of your company and to enhance your personal influence and career in positive ways, and 2) To help protect you from others who are trying to exert their influence over you in ways detrimental to your company and/or you personally.

Enhancing Your Resources Worksheet

Personal Attribute	Notes/Actions
Money/Budget	
Equipment	
Location	
Documentation	
Business Process	
Software	
Intellectual Property	
Physical Access	
Organizational Access	
Personal Connections	
Information	

UNDERSTANDING WORKPLACE SITUATIONAL INFLUENCE

If you understand the knowledge required to put you on equal or greater footing with those whom you are trying to influence, you can make the required learning a priority or hire an expert to help.

~Eric Bloom

Situational influence, as the name suggests, is the level of influence at the current moment. Historically, this topic is heavily discussed and analyzed in marketing and psychology. This chapter provides a brief overview of situational influence from these two important perspectives, then expands on them into my area of study: influence between individuals in the workplace.

In the marketing world, situational influence is a deeply researched, well-known, and respected area of research, focused on producing best practices for creating an environment in which customers buy products in physical locations, and more recently, internet-based retail outlets. It considers customer-based buying factors, such as the product's physical surroundings, customers' social interaction with others, the emotional reason to buy, immediacy of product availability, and other related factors. The next time you walk into a store and wonder why you are tempted to buy products you originally had no intention of purchasing, it's because of thoughtful implementation of this area of research.

In the psychology world, situational influence is also a deeply researched, well-known, and respected area. The intent is to understand and assist patients in improving their lives, dealing with illness, and coping with life's other difficulties. For example, the Actor-Partner Interdependence Model analyzes the relationship and interdependency between two individuals, often when one is dealing with an issue such as depression and the other is the spouse or another family member, with the goal of enhancing patient and family wellbeing.

In the workplace, situational influence combines and expands on these two previous areas of study in the following way: It includes what makes people want to "buy" and the "interdependency" between coworkers in the office. The combination of these two factors provides the "How to do it" and "Why it works" when influencing others within the workplace.

WORKPLACE SITUATIONAL INFLUENCE

In the workplace, all influence is situational. Understanding your relative level of knowledge and control compared to others is key in assessing your ability to influence them. Your workplace situational influence is comprised of two main factors:

- Situational knowledge

- Situational audience

Situational knowledge is how much you know about the topic currently being discussed. For example, an organic farmer may not have much influence over an upcoming bake sale at their child's school, but if the organizers decide to produce more natural options, the farmer's opinion becomes more influential.

Situational audience refers to your level of influential-power related to the specific person or people you are trying to influence. There are two types of situational audience: organizational and social.

> **Organizational influence** refers to your relative level of organizational power, as compared to the individual, group, or audience you are trying to influence. For example, if you are a project manager, you will have greater influence over those working on your team than you will over your boss or the key project stakeholders who will be evaluating your project's success.

Social influence refers to situations with no formal organizational structure, for example, when talking to friends or speaking in a public forum, like a professional association or industry group. Generally speaking, your level of influence depends upon your audience's level of interest. They may exhibit interest, neutrality, or reluctance toward your project. For example, if you are rolling out a new travel expense reporting system within your company, those who don't travel as part of their jobs won't care, those who don't like the previous process will be interested, and those who like the current system will be reluctant.

USING THE WORKPLACE SITUATIONAL INFLUENCE CONCEPT TO YOUR ADVANTAGE

The concepts of situational knowledge and situational audience can be used to your advantage in various ways, including:

Picking your battles

Understanding your relative level of knowledge and organizational power can help you decide which office scenarios (for example, negotiations, conflicts, projects, presentations, etc.) to embrace and which to avoid. Making the correct decisions can minimize your business risk, steer you away from internal political landmines, and allow you to strategically select the projects and interpersonal interactions that play to your strengths, not your weaknesses.

Preparing for meetings

The lower your organizational power, the greater your need to gain influence and control using situational knowledge. In other words, if you cannot control the room using political strength, you can still control it using knowledge. If you can't be the boss, be the expert.

Knowing when to request assistance

If influence is required to achieve a specific outcome, and you have neither the organizational power nor the needed level of topic knowledge, bring a higher-ranking employee, your boss for example, or a subject matter expert who can talk on your behalf.

Detecting when you are being set up for a fall

Presenting to a group when you have neither the organizational power nor a greater topical knowledge than the audience is a recipe for disaster. A strong understanding of your situational knowledge and audience helps you avoid these types of situations or, at a minimum, warns you that peril may be ahead, allowing you to be properly prepared to protect yourself.

Prioritizing personal learning

When you understand the knowledge required to put you on equal or greater footing with those whom you are trying to influence, you can prioritize the order of your personal training classes, internet research, and other knowledge-gathering activities.

The chapter on Calculating Your Influence Power Rating explains how to quantify your situational knowledge and situational audience.

IPR ATTRIBUTE SURVEY RESULTS

The data show that the number one attribute affecting office influence, above all others, in all demographic categories is "trustworthiness."

~Eric Bloom and The Data

To assist with the research for this book, a survey was created, in cooperation with the University of Northern Colorado. The survey assessed the importance of the seventy-four influence attributes included in the IPR calculation. Each attribute was rated using the following scale:

1 = Not important

2 = Somewhat unimportant

3 = Somewhat important

4 = Important

5 = Very important

The research's goal was to learn:

- The influential importance of each attribute

- The relative importance of the five attribute categories included in the IPR calculation

- The importance of each attribute by job type and other demographics

- What future research should be done based upon these initial findings

The knowledge gained from this initial research is currently being used in many ways, including:

- Validating the inclusion of each attribute within the IPR calculation

- Using it to maximize the value of advice provided in Part 3 of this book

- Providing valuable, unique information to our training class students and those attending my keynote speeches

- Creating weighting factors for the IPR within the calculation of our "online Office Influence Assessment" offered via our website to our students and my keynote participants

- Developing the core research to better understand and measure influence dynamics within the workplace

The following results are based upon survey results available at the time of this book's printing. The survey and related research will be ongoing.

The word "influence" means many things to many people. Therefore, to properly understand the results, you must first understand the context of the survey's questions.

Office influence is the ability to move a person's thinking, actions, and/or decisions in a way that advances your business objectives.

As you can see by this definition, office influence specifically addresses only influence within the workplace. While many commonalities may exist with other types of influence, such as that within families, when buying products, or politicians lobbying for your vote, they are outside our area of study.

To date, there have been some interesting results, some of which were expected and some of which, at least for me, were rather eye-opening.

The data show that the number one attribute affecting office influence, in all demographic categories, was "trustworthiness." Although other top ten attributes varied in their ranking, "trustworthiness" was always first.

The overall top ten were:

	Attribute	Average Value[1]
1.	Trustworthiness	4.88
2.	Active listening	4.77
3.	Leading by example	4.62
4.	Accountability	4.61
5.	Follow-Through	4.60
6.	Commitment	4.60
7.	Experience	4.59
8.	Emotional intelligence	4.56
9.	Vision	4.54
10.	Asking purposeful questions	4.53

Future analytical research will ascertain why these attributes are in the top ten. In the meantime, I'd like to provide my thoughts based on anecdotal evidence collected during many years in the workplace and as an instructor and speaker on the topic.

1. **Trustworthiness:** I believe this attribute came in first because if you trust someone, you are willing to let your guard down and internalize the other person's information, advice, and insights. This internalization causes you to seriously consider their suggestions, even if you ultimately decide not to take them.

2. **Active listening:** People want to be heard and understood. The active listening process includes visual and verbal cues that you are paying attention to the speaker. Additionally, active listening provides you

---

[1] "Average value" is based on the 1–5 scale described at the beginning of this chapter.

with the information needed to influence someone in a way that is meaningful to them, not you.

3. **Leading by example:** In general, it is much easier to influence others by saying "Do as I do," rather than "Don't do as I do. Do as I say." I think this stems from our collective memory as children wanting to emulate people we respected.

4. **Accountability:** People tend to appreciate and respect those who are accountable for their actions, willing to admit their mistakes, and quietly accept praise for their accomplishments. This accountability is perceived as inner strength, conviction, fairness, and authenticity.

5. **Follow-Through:** We all respect people who follow through on tasks they agreed to take on and promises made to others, and who take their assigned responsibilities seriously. This admiration provides the opportunity to influence others.

6. **Commitment:** When someone is truly committed and driven toward a specific business goal, it's infectious; others want to get involved and become part of the energy (and success).

7. **Experience:** Professional and personal experiences, both successes and failures, create learned wisdom and facilitate mastery. For example, all things being equal, would you be more likely to take advice on starting a business from a successful serial entrepreneur or someone who has read a book or two on "How to start your own company"?

8. **Emotional intelligence:** I think emotional intelligence is a fundamental building block for all types of human interaction, including influence, negotiation, and conflict resolution. I was surprised that it came in at #8 and not #2, right after trustworthiness. My gut feeling is that those who marked it lower have not yet studied its importance and power.

9. **Vision:** People like to follow others who can articulate a clear and desirable vision. A vision allows them to participate in something bigger than themselves. In the workplace, this is coupled with the employee's personal agenda of increased compensation, career advancement, and resume-based accomplishments.

10. **Asking purposeful questions:** The ability to ask purposeful questions is one of my favorite types of influence, so I was glad it squeezed into the top ten. As described in Chapter 6: Influential Communication, a correctly posed question allows you to guide people toward a desired outcome. It is also a great way to make them feel ownership of your idea.

I also found it particularly interesting that the following attributes scored near or at the bottom of the list:

Degrees: While a college degree has great value from the knowledge gained, professional contacts made, and credentials needed to get a great job, it holds little value when trying to influence your coworkers. After starting the job, the importance of the college degree fades away and is replaced by job performance, emotional intelligence, and other work-related factors.

Budget/Money: Controlling the budget certainly provides an advantage over people who don't since the person holding the purse strings can say "No, I won't fund your initiative." However, just because you control the money does not guarantee you can get others to say "yes" and work toward your vision.

Job title: While a job title has many professional advantages, the data show it does not carry much weight when trying to influence your peers or others within the workplace. However, based on my experience, I believe that a job title can be an influential factor when dealing with vendors and customers. However, this influence can be diminished if they begin to believe it's a shallow label, not carrying the clout it suggests.

Awards: Although the data have not proven this to be true, I believe this attribute will move much higher within certain professions, like art, entertainment, and scientific research, where awards are viewed as a litmus test of achievement and respectability among peers.

Lastly, a few attributes were also tied to specific professions, including:

Certifications: While certifications scored below average in the overall population, it was within the top ten in professions such as Project Management, where certifications are highly respected, widely achieved, and an avenue to employment and upward mobility.

Intellectual Property: That this did not score higher was another surprise. My hypothesis is that because employees have access to their company's intellectual property, when needed, as part of their jobs, there is no influence-based advantage. It will be interesting to analyze this from the vendor's point of view, because vendors use their intellectual property as a key marketing asset and an advantage over their competition. This type of analysis is currently outside our area of study, but it may be included in the future.

Industry and association activism: I'm a big supporter of industry associations. In fact, I am a member of four associations: National Speakers Association (NSA), Project Management Institute (PMI), Association for Talent Development (ATD), and the International Institute of Business Analysis (IIBA). It is my firm belief that professional associations enhance members' skills and knowledge by providing state-of-the-art development resources in their professional areas, which helps advance the participants' careers. I also believe these types of associations enhance their professional disciplines through the combination of topical research, professional certifications, and the collective wisdom that manifests when likeminded professionals meet in groups and compare best practices. My future analysis will include the study of influential power in professions where association activism is highly respected.

The survey also asked what additional attributes should be added to the survey. The data showed that the following items should be included in our future research because of their important effect on office influence.

These attributes are:

- Empathetic

- Calm

- Transparent

- Humorous

- Authentic

- Courageous

- Creative

While these new attributes are contained in the book's text, they are not included in this chapter's survey results due to insufficient data quantity.

Future survey results, findings, and interpretations will be posted on my blogs and in my other professional correspondence as they become available.

[PART 3]

USING INFLUENCE TO YOUR ADVANTAGE

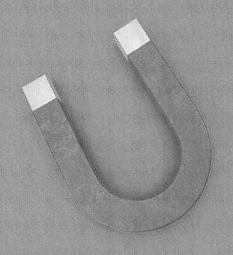

USING INFLUENCE TO YOUR ADVANTAGE

In the introduction, I made a bold statement about influence, stating that, "Every interpersonal endeavor includes an aspect of influence." In negotiation, you're influencing people to move closer to your point of view. In change management, you're influencing people to do something different. In conflict resolution, you're influencing people or organizations to resolve their issues and get along. The list goes on and on.

This third and final section gives light to this bold statement by providing specific instructions on how the various influence concepts, techniques, tips, and tricks discussed in Parts 1 and 2 can be used to enhance your success in various workplace-related, interpersonal activities.

The chapters that follow concentrate on the use of influence within a specific workplace activity:

- Influence-Based Negotiating

- Influence-Based Organizational Change

- Influence-Based Delegating

- Influence-Based Conflict Resolution

- Influence-Based Presentation Success

- Influence-Based Project Management

- Influence-Based Leadership

Each chapter in Part 3 contains a worksheet designed to help organize and implement the influence-based techniques discussed.

INFLUENCE-BASED NEGOTIATING

If you can foresee with whom you will be negotiating, you can set the stage to influence them well in advance of the negotiation.

~Eric Bloom

Every interpersonal endeavor includes an aspect of influence. When negotiating, you are influencing an individual person or group to move closer to your point of view. This chapter combines influence-based and negotiation-based concepts into a single activity.

ENHANCING YOUR POTENTIAL INFLUENCE IN FUTURE NEGOTIATIONS

If, based on your business experience and understanding of future work activities, you have the ability to identify the specific people with whom you will be negotiating, you can set the stage to influence that negotiation well in advance of the actual negotiation process.

As an important note of caution, for these preparatory activities to be successful, you must ensure that your subjects cannot connect your current influence-based activities and the future negotiation. If a connection is made, it can harm both your negotiating position and your professional brand.

Influencer: Personal connection

Begin to establish a trusted relationship with the opposing negotiators. It will be mutually beneficial for both sides for talking more honestly and openly. You don't have to be friends, even though that would be nice, but you need to create a positive working relationship.

Think about it from your personal experience. You are more easily influenced by someone you trust, and conversely, it is easier to influence someone who trusts you. So, you are more likely to reach a negotiated agreement with someone you believe will hold up their end of the deal and will not try to take advantage of your goodwill

Influencer: Use Observation to Understand a Person's Interests
You can gain interesting insights into a person's interests and persona by seeing their office space. This is a technique often used by salespeople to:

- Find conversational topics.

- Find a common bond (common interest).

- Gain an understanding of the prospect's:
    » Values (pictures or awards from non-profit organizations)
    » Priorities (pictures of family on their desk)
    » Interests (world maps, sports memorabilia)
    » Level of competitiveness (trophies or pictures of personal triumphs)
    » Educational background (diplomas or memorabilia from their alma mater)
    » Topics of literary interests (books on a bookshelf)
    » Current literary interests (books on the desk)

Salespeople use this information to create a common bond with the prospect. This bond helps build trust, likeability, influence, and hopefully, a very profitable, long-term relationship.

You can use this same technique to gain understanding of the people with whom you will be negotiating, requesting support from, or influencing in some way in the future.

Influencer: Reciprocity
Reciprocity, as you may recall from the chapter on Cialdini's Six Principles of Influence, means when you do something good for someone,

they will feel a social obligation to do something good for you.

You can use this concept to your advantage by, as the opportunity presents itself, doing small, nice things for those with whom you will be negotiating. For example, if you receive an unsolicited email about a topic the company's chief information officer may find interesting, forward it, simply saying, "I saw this and thought of you." This small action will build goodwill toward you and instill a small feeling of obligation to return the favor.

Example tactics include:

- You receive an unsolicited email about a topic they may find interesting; forward it saying, "I saw this and thought of you."

- Introduce a potential new client to a vendor.

- Tell the person's manager about the great job the person is doing.

Influencer: Liking

Liking, another topic in Cialdini's Six Principles of Influence, states that people are more likely to be influenced by people they like. Therefore, if you get those future negotiation partners to like you, you will be better able to influence them during negotiation. Interestingly, the previously mentioned Reciprocity Influencer also has the benefit of getting people to like you just because you thought of them and did something nice.

Potential tactics include:

- Building your "Reciprocity Bank," which can increase liking.

- Finding common interests between you and the other person. (You both work out at lunch in the company's gym, perhaps.)

Influencer: Consistency/Currency Combination

The concept of influence consistency (also discussed in the chapter on Cialdini) is getting someone to do a little of something now, so you can get them to more of it later. When you combine consistency with Cohen-Bradford's concept of influence currencies, and find currency that is important to the person, like position-related recognition, then influencing them a little now, by recognizing their accomplishments and abilities, will condition them to be influenced using the same method in the future.

As an added benefit, this type of influence currency also adds to liking.

Potential tactical steps include:

1. Find the person's influence currencies.

2. Provide this currency in little doses over time.

3. Get the person conditioned to receiving this currency.

4. After the negotiation begins, provide currency in small doses during the negotiation in return for small negotiation favors.

These steps are designed to be similar to how casinos influence people to continue to play slot machines by providing ongoing small rewards.

Influencer: Inverted Influence

When using the Inverted Influence strategy, you seemingly allow yourself to be influenced by another person specifically to gain their attention, favor, trust, and support. As mentioned earlier in the book, I don't like this strategy. I consider it both manipulative and disingenuous, but it can be an effective strategy, nevertheless. Also, be very careful that others are not using this tactic on you. It works because it feels nice to believe you are able to influence others.

From a negotiation perspective, gaining favor in advance makes it easier to influence others once you begin negotiating.

NEGOTIATION PREPARATIONS

Preparation for an upcoming negotiation, after the topic and players are defined, should include everything previously discussed regarding future negotiations, but tailored specifically to your target audience.

Your preparations should also include taking stock of your Core Influence Characteristics, Situational Knowledge, and Situational Audience, which are the three primary components of the IPR calculation. Understanding your own IPR and trying to understand the IPR of those with whom you are negotiating can provide key insights into:

- Your influence strength relative to the other party.

- How to best prepare yourself prior to the start of negotiation.

- The relative influence of the people in the other party's negotiating team, if there is more than one person.

This concept is described below in detail.

Influencer: Influence Power Rating (IPR)—Your IPR
You can use the IPR calculation to assess your core influence characteristics and, if time allows, enhance a specific characteristic that could increase your influence during the negotiation. Examples include:

- If your boss agrees to support you, then your delegated authority is increased.

- Bringing approved budget dollars to the table increases your ability to dictate the agreement's conditions.

- Researching the topic of discussion increases your situational knowledge.

Influencer: Influence Power Rating (IPR)—Others IPR
The IPR can also be used to assess the influence of those with whom you are negotiating. When using the IPR this way, based on the information you know or can research, perform your assessment in two ways:

1. Compare their team against your team (or you against the other person in a one-on-one negotiation).

2. If the opposition consists of multiple people, use the IPR to identify and then assess the individual with the most influence and the team's ultimate decision maker.

The first comparison provides insight into who has the upper hand in the negotiation from a personal strength perspective. Note, however, that this is only one of many factors that determine which team has the upper hand. That said, it's still an interesting data point.

The second comparison gives you insight into the best way to gain an advantage over the other party. Knowing who the opposition leader is allows you to focus your negotiation and influence energy. This is a common technique used by salespeople to help identify and then persuade decision-makers.

USING INFLUENCE TECHNIQUES DURING THE NEGOTIATION PROCESS

There are many traditional influence techniques you can use to get the upper hand during negotiations. These include:

- Threatening to walk away from the deal.

- Pushing the other party to make a quick decision.

- Intimidation (yuck—don't use this one).

- Nibbling (asking for a little extra value in anticipation of closing the deal).

- Crying poor (saying you only have a certain amount to spend).

- Beginning negotiations with a second party (as in entertaining a competing bid for the business).

- Dividing a large vendor proposal into small pieces, and negotiating each smaller task's price.

In addition to these traditional negotiation techniques, other influence-based techniques you can use to improve your negotiation outcomes include:

Influencer: Problem/Vision Statements
Clearly define the business problem the negotiation is addressing and a future vision (your future vision) of how to solve the problem. If you can get the other party to agree with your vision, then your negotiating position will be greatly improved because all future discussions will be based on your vision.

The Problem/Vision statements you create could use the following templates:

Problem Definition
The problem is _____, resulting in _____, thereby having the consequence of _____.

Problem End State (Vision)
It would be great if _____, allowing us to _____, thereby having the advantage of _____.

Influencer: Taking logistical control
Logistical control is about managing negotiation-related activities, such as emailing the meeting invitations and reserving the conference room. Taking this control puts you in a pseudo-leadership role over the other negotiators.

When you take logistical control of the negotiation by scheduling the meetings, selecting the location, ordering snacks, and paying for lunch, you set a precedent. Once this precedent is set, roles are defined, and it positions you to drive the pace, location, agenda, and other related items of the negotiations to your advantage.

This also has a second advantage of creating agreement momentum in your favor. For example, try to get the other party to say (in this order):

1. Yes, we can meet in your office.

2. Yes, next Tuesday at 1 p.m. is fine.

3. Yes, thank you for bringing in lunch. I'll have a chicken sandwich please.

4. Yes, I would like a cup of coffee. Thank you.

5. Yes, I'll agree to your contract terms.

As an added benefit, if they appreciate your efforts in planning the meeting and bringing lunch, then you are also creating a sense of reciprocity.

Influencer: Location selection
Try to schedule the physical location for negotiations where you will have greater personal power—for example, in your office rather than the other person's. The sports equivalent is having the home court advantage. This technique also enhances your ability to take logistical control of the negotiation process.

Potential tactics include:

- Schedule the physical location of all meetings.

- Develop a routine of meeting in your location.

- Use location selection to establish logistical control.

Influencer: You should write the contract

Given the opportunity, you (your team) should write the contact. You must be fair, but when you write the contract, the negotiation begins with everything you want on the table. Like selecting the meeting's location, this technique also enhances your ability to take logistical control of the negotiation process.

Tactics of this type include:

1. Start by using your company's Non-Disclosure Agreement (NDA). (They are all basically the same anyway.)

2. Speak with your internal legal group to make sure they are willing to write it.

3. Offer to write the contract.

4. Have the other side suggest changes, and then incorporate them into the contract.

Influencer: Accepting constructive feedback

If the other person gives you feedback on your proposal, suggestions, or anything else, use this to your advantage through leading by example. Appreciate the feedback and show your willingness to consider it. This positions you to give feedback, when the time is right; that subtlety moves the other person toward your position. Because you previously accepted their feedback, they will now be more likely to accept yours.

One caution: If you accept their advice too often without them accepting yours, this could create a precedent and cultural norm that is hard to overcome. In fact, you are trying to create the reverse.

Potential tactics if the other person gives you feedback or suggestions include:

- Truly appreciate the feedback.

- Show your willingness to consider their ideas.

- Potentially act on the feedback if you think it's to your future advantage.

Influencer: Taking the moral high ground
If you can find a way to align your negotiation interests with a greater good, for example being good for the company, then it becomes more difficult for the other person to push their personal agenda because it comes across as less worthy and less moral.

Potential tactics include tying your negotiating position to:

- Organizational objectives

- Company values (environmental protection, local outreach, etc.)

- Company wellbeing (increased profit)

- Social cause important to the other party

Influencer: Show gratitude
Gratitude is one of the Cohen-Bradford currencies. If you are negotiating with someone who likes to be acknowledged for having done something nice, thanking them is not only the right thing to do, but it is also to your influence-benefit. If you feed their personal need to be thanked, they will not only like you more, but they will also be more likely to give you additional favors.

Tactics of this type include:

- Say "Thank you" or "Thanks. I appreciate it" when deserved.

- Thank the person in public or by copying their manager on an email.

- Describe their good deed in a meeting as an example for others.

Influencer: Be a problem solver

As problems arise during the negotiation—even little things like not being able to find the flipchart—proactively be the one to solve them. By doing so, you create a precedent and micro-culture that features you as the group's problem solver. This will have a great influence-advantage when negotiation-based issues arise because people will look to you to solve issues, thus allowing you to solve issues to your advantage.

- Potential tactics as small problems that may arise include:

- Finding flipchart paper during a meeting

- Inviting a subject matter expert to help on a specific topic

- Having an extra pen in case someone forgot theirs

Influencer: Presentation excellence

Never underestimate the power of making a good presentation or clearly articulating an important message. People will be impressed by your ability to present your thoughts and, as a result, will be more likely to be swayed by you.

If you don't consider yourself a good public speaker, look into workshops or Toastmasters International or some other training. Public speaking is one of the most important things you can do to enhance your career.

Influencer: Be calm during adversity

When discussions get heated, people naturally turn to the person who can show calming strength and conviction. If this person is you, when the negotiation becomes tense, you can be the voice of reason, civility, and professional decorum. When people turn to you, you can influence the players' actions and the direction of the discussion, which, of course, is toward your interests.

Influencer: Storytelling

Carefully crafted stories that include facts, emotion, and vision can influence others to follow your negotiation positions. The story has to resonate with them personally by touching their values, business needs, professional aspirations, sense of fairness, empathy, ethics, or other related business/personal connections.

Tactics of this type include:

1. Gaining an understanding of the other party's values, negotiation needs, and wants

2. Defining a story that forwards your negotiation goals

3. Crafting the story in a way that resonates with their:

    • Business needs
    • Personal values
    • Professional aspirations
    • Sense of fairness, empathy, and ethics

4. Practice, practice, practice

Influence-Based Negotiating Influencers Worksheet

Project/Initiative Name: _____

Negotiating Influencers	Other Negotiating Party	Notes/Actions
Enhancing your potential influence in future negotiations		
Personal connection		
Use Observation to Understand Others' Interests		
Reciprocity		
Liking		
Consistency/Currency Combination		
Inverted Influence		
Negotiation Preparations		
Your IPR		
Others' IPR		
Using influence techniques during the negotiation process		
Problem/Vision Statements		

Influence-Based Negotiating Influencers Worksheet

Negotiating Influencers	Other Negotiating Party	Notes/Actions
Using influence techniques during the negotiation process		
Taking logistical control		
Location selection		
Writing the contract		
Accepting constructive feedback		
Taking the moral high ground		
Showing gratitude		
Being a problem solver		
Presentation excellence		
Being calm during adversity		
Storytelling		

INFLUENCE-BASED ORGANIZATIONAL CHANGE

If you want to truly understand something, try to change it.

~Kurt Lewin

This chapter combines influence-based and change-based concepts into a single activity. I will begin by giving a high-level overview of the ITML Institute's ERICA Change Management Framework, then provide examples of how to assist each framework component via the use of influence-based techniques and concepts.

While reading this chapter, view it from two perspectives. First, as the title suggests, how can you use influence-based concepts to enhance your organizational change activities? Second, how can you use the influence techniques in this chapter to your professional advantage?

Figure 22.1

The five components of the ERICA Organizational Change Framework are:

E: Environment

Organizational change is framed within its environment. It is the reasons and circumstances for the change. The reason for the change may be an internal or external factor. Internal factors include new leadership, a merger or acquisition, significant change in profitability (+/-), or other circumstances. External change is caused by shifts in the economy, technological innovations, legislation, new competitors, or other issues outside the company's control.

The urgency of change is how quickly the change must happen. There may be a crisis to avoid like an organizational catastrophe, an immediate shift in strategy or competitive landscape, or a new opportunity.

The impact of the change is the holistic effect it will have on the organization, namely cultural, procedural, structural, or technological.

Lastly, the scope of the change is the extent of the effect on people and organizational silos. This scope could be a single individual, department, division, or the overall company.

R: Resources

Based upon the reason, urgency, impact, and scope of the change, the resources needed to implement the change may include people, funding, and/or senior level managerial support.

I: Individuals

Organizations are often conceptualized as having a life of their own—they are their own living creatures. To a certain extent, that may be true. However, under the covers, individual people are making the decisions and doing the work. Therefore, implementing change within any organization, regardless of size, is done by influencing individuals to comply with organizational change. To change the organization, you must use techniques that will modify the activities, skills, mindsets, etc. of individual employees to the extent needed to implement vision.

C: Culture

Organizations have personalities just like people, but because they are bigger, they call it culture. This, in many cases, is the hardest thing to change. It requires a collective mindset shift by all those in the culture being modified. This change may cause some people to leave and others to thrive during this transition period.

Because each organizational silo has its own microculture, cultural change is extremely complex. For example, the culture within the sales department is most likely different from the culture within the accounting department. As a result, if the cultural change is company-wide, then even though the cultural goal is the same for both departments, the tactics needed to implement it may be very different.

A: Actions

The actions consist of change management plans, the execution of the plans, and measurement of the expected and unexpected results. To the extent possible, these change action plans should be prioritized and resourced following the company's standard prioritization process and performed using your existing project management methodologies.

The ERICA framework is described to this level of detail because, to influence something, you must first have a detailed understanding of what you are trying to influence. This understanding is the foundation for where, when, and what kind of influence can be used to maximize its effect.

With the ERICA framework explained, let's discuss the influence-based techniques that can be used to facilitate each framework component.

UNDERSTANDING THE CHANGING ENVIRONMENT

The circumstances causing the need for change are generally dictated by external forces; therefore, it is unlikely you can do anything to modify the external change environment. If this is not the case, your ability to influence the reason, vision, urgency, impact, and/or scope of the change can have a great effect on the:

- Resources needed

- Individuals affected

- Cultural shifts

- Action plan activities

Therefore, if you are able to influence the environment, do so first because of the dramatic effect it has on all the other factors within the ERICA framework. Specific, influence-based techniques are not included in this section because the reasons for organizational change are so broad in nature. When considering ways to influence the reason for the change, consider the full array of change concepts, strategies, and techniques described within this book.

GATHERING NEEDED RESOURCES

Influencer: Delegated authority
Delegated authority is using another person's organizational clout as your own to increase your influence and/or authority. For example, if the company's chief financial officer (CFO) instructs you to replace the existing budgeting system with newer, more feature-rich software, then you are acting under the CFO's authority. This authority can then be used to gain the needed information, support, and funding to complete the project. Your goal in using this newfound clout is to use it sparingly, only as needed, and not as a bully pulpit for your personal advantage.

Potential tactics include:

- Gaining the support of senior executives in the organization where the change will occur.

- Work your way down in the organization, from SVP to VP, to director, and so on, continually going from manager to employee.

Influencer: Motivation through vision (pull-based influence)
You can enlist people to directly help you or provide their resources

(budget, information, people, etc.) by sharing your vision with them in a way that makes them want to help you. In effect, you are letting others have things your way.

Potential tactics include:

- **For getting people:** Explaining to the manager and employee how it's good for the employee's career to be involved in your change project.

- **For getting a budget:** Explain the high potential return on investment (ROI) on the invested money.

- **For information or data:** Explain how sharing their data is good for the company (taking the high road).

Influencer: Reciprocity

When using reciprocity to get needed resources, ideally, if you have the opportunity to plan ahead, find a way to build your reciprocity bank by:

- Targeting the specific people from whom you'll need resources as part of your change activities.

- Offering your resources for one of their projects.

- Prioritizing a pet project important to the person you will asking for resources at a later time.

Influencer: Consistency

The concept of influence consistency is: If you can get someone to do a little of something, you can get them to do more of the same sometime later. Therefore, if you begin by asking for a small resource commitment, it may be easier for you to attain more substantial resources in the future if the person thinks the resources related to your first request were used wisely.

Potential tactics include:

- (As previously mentioned regarding reciprocity) targeting the specific people from whom you'll need resources to support your change activities.

- Beginning by asking them for advice related to your project. When they provide you their insights, this is the first step in their "consistency chain." They gave you a little of their time and thought, and next time, they may give you people or budget dollars. Also, by asking their advice, it gives them a small, vested interest in your project's success.

- If you need more than one type of resource from the same person, carefully consider the order in which to ask for these resources. For example, if you need people, data, and money, you may want to go from easiest to hardest (data, money, people), from hardest to easiest (people, money, data), or simply ask for all three at once.

Influencer: Finding mutual gain

If possible, find a way to implement your change so it is also of value to the person you are trying to influence. This way, they are not just giving resources to you—they are using their resources for their own gain, which happens to be to your advantage as well.

Potential tactical steps:

1. Access the value of the change to the person you are targeting for resources.

2. If the change is truly of no value or negative value to this person, use a different influence approach.

3. If the change is of value, clearly explain the benefits of the change from the person's perspective by explaining the end-state of the change once it's implemented.

4. Once they have "bought into" the change and believe it will be good for them, then work together on how to combine your resources to produce the desired end-state.

Influencer: Direct request

While all the previously listed influence techniques can be very effective, sometimes the best, most straightforward way to gain the needed resources is simply to ask. I saved this one for last because using any of the previously listed techniques first makes "the ask" a little easier and a lot more successful.

CHANGING INDIVIDUAL MINDSETS

Influencer: Emotional intelligence

Each person looks at change from a unique perspective. The better you understand their perspective, the easier it will be for you to influence them. This is empathy, which is a key component of emotional intelligence. If you have never studied emotional intelligence, I strongly suggest that you do. It will provide insight into how to empathize with others and use this understanding of people to your professional advantage.

Potential tools for gaining an understanding of others include:

- Asking open-ended questions.

- Active listening.

- Truly caring about what others have to say.

Influencer: Personal Connection

All interpersonal interactions, including influence, change, negotiation, and more, are enhanced if the people interacting have previously created a positive, trusting, interpersonal connection. This allows you to begin forming a positive relationship prior to discussing the issues, implications, and challenges of the change ahead.

Potential tactics include:

- Meeting with the person for coffee as a friendly introduction.

- If you cannot meet in person, doing a video chat, which will give you a chance to see each other face-to-face.

Influencer: Storytelling
Stories, if told correctly, bring together information, settings, actions, emotions, and other factors involving many parts of your brain. This is the reason stories are so memorable and persuasive. Storytelling can be used to your advantage because you are not just telling them about some change, but showing them what life will look like once this change is in place—it's much more interesting than a list of bullet points or numeric data.

This story should include:

- The current situation.

- Why the change needs to be made.

- The desired outcome.

- The process for getting there.

This will give people a holistic understanding of the change, and ideally, gain their support in the process.

Influencer: Leading questions
A leading question is posed with the intent of soliciting a specific answer or action. You can use these types of questions to point people toward the change you would like to facilitate. In effect, their answers will convince them to go along, or even help, with the change you are implementing.

Example questions include:

- Based on the company's new change initiative, what advantages do you see for your department?

- Did you know the company's new (changed) vendor management policy will make it easier for you to buy office supplies?

Influencer: Social proof
People often look at the behavior of others to make decisions. Therefore, referring to respected people within the organization who have accepted the change can be used to influence those who are more reluctant.

Example tactics include:

- Identify an organization's influential people first. Get them to accept the change, and then use their internal influence to get others to agree.

- List competitive companies that use the same software, vendor, process, etc.

- List industry thought leaders who are suggesting your type of change is required to remain competitive.

CHANGING ORGANIZATIONAL CULTURE

Influencer: Understanding microcultures
It's important that you understand not only your company's overall culture, but also the embedded microcultures and/or organizational silos of the departments that will be affected by the change.

Example tactic:

If the change you are implementing is a new, company-wide process, you may need to describe it to the salesforce in a different way than to the accounting department, because their internal departmental cultures, goals, and challenges are different.

Influencer: Statement Repetition

Statement repetition, in an organizational change sense, is the process of repeating your message through multiple avenues on an ongoing basis with the goal of employees/members internalizing the message.

This concept can be used to help facilitate your required change by identifying the people who should be reached and the multiple ways they can be contacted via their natural work flow.

Example tactics include:

- Place the message of change on people's computer/laptop wallpapers or login screens.

- Hang posters in the hallways.

- Place a small sign on everyone's desk.

- Place a large sign at the office entrance and/or other similar locations.

The more people who see your signs, the more likely they will move toward the change through osmosis and a feeling of inevitability.

Influencer: Senior management support

All organizational change requires the support of the organization's leadership. Without it, there is no motivation, resources, time, or financial incentive to implement the change.

One of your first actions, when trying to implement change, is to assess managerial support for the change. If management requests the change, then support is assumed. If the change is being pushed upon local management from outside their location—for example, the implementation of a new, company-wide business process—then you must begin your efforts by influencing local management to assist in the change process. Without this local management support, your project will likely fail.

ACTION PLANNING, IMPLEMENTATION, AND MEASUREMENT

Action plans, the execution of those plans, and measurement of change results should follow standard, internal project management methodologies.

To best understand how influence can be used when managing projects of all types, please refer to Chapter 26: Influence-Based Project Management.

Influence-Based Organizational Change Worksheet

Project/Initiative Name: _____

Change Influencers	Other Party	Notes/Actions
Gathering needed resources		
Delegated authority		
Motivation through vision (Pull-based influence)		
Reciprocity		
Consistency		
Finding mutual gain		
Direct Request		
Changing individual mindsets		
Emotional intelligence		
Personal connection		
Storytelling		
Leading questions		
Social proof		
Changing organizational culture		
Understanding microcultures		
Statement repetition		
Senior management support		

INFLUENCE-BASED DELEGATING

One delegated action should always provide two or more business benefits.

~Eric Bloom

Widen your view on delegation from just asking those who work for you to perform tasks to asking all those working within your company, plus vendors, customers, and all others. This widened perspective allows you to look at both delegation and influence more holistically.

The process of task delegation follows the same set of steps; the difference is getting people to agree to accept the delegated task as their own. For example, when delegating to one of your staff, it's your job to assign them tasks and their job to do those tasks. However, this is not the case if that individual is a dotted-line employee, customer, peer, or your boss.

This chapter will highlight the delegation process and how to use influence to motivate each of these resources to complete the task.

ONE DELEGATION, TWO OR MORE BUSINESS BENEFITS

When thinking about delegation, always look beyond the task itself and consider what other benefits can be derived from your delegated actions. For example, if you are delegating to a member of your staff, are they enhancing their skills, thereby providing them with additional upward visibility, increasing their motivation, or preparing them for promotion? If you're delegating to a customer, are you also strengthening the customer relationship, enhancing customer satisfaction, and/or training the customer to be more self-reliant?

If you consider these secondary and tertiary benefits, it will be easier for you to influence others to perform the needed task.

EIGHT-STEP PROCESS TO MAXIMIZE DELEGATION EFFECTIVENESS

Like all leadership activities, delegation must be done in a thoughtful, ethical, and forward-thinking manner. To that end, consider the following steps when delegating tasks to your staff, contractors, vendors, customers, and others.

1. **Clearly define what can and cannot be delegated:** As a manager, be mindful of what should and should not be delegated. For example, specific tasks may involve proprietary information that should not be shared at your staff's organizational level. As a second example, there are tasks your team members may not be qualified to perform, thus setting them up for failure. Lastly, don't just dump unwanted tasks onto your staff to get the item off your plate. Your team will eventually figure this out, and it will hurt your credibility as their manager.

   On the positive side, delegation can be a powerful tool to maximize your team's productivity, enhance their skills, help them grow professionally, and free you up to perform higher level tasks. All that said, make sure you are delegating the right tasks for the right reasons.

2. **Create a delegation prioritization plan:** Once you know what to delegate, your next step is developing a plan outlining which tasks should be delegated to whom. When determining who gets a task, consider the following:

   - Who is fully qualified to perform the task?

   - Who could perform the task with proper instruction and mentoring, with the goal of enhancing their skills?

   - Who should not be given the task because of their professional weaknesses or other reasons?

- Who deserves the task based on seniority, past performance, and other relevant considerations?

- How visible and important is the task to your department and/or company?

Delegating the right tasks to the right people is not always easy and/or popular, but if you do it with transparency, fairness, consistency, and for the good of the company, your staff will learn to respect your decisions, even if, from time to time, they don't like how a specific task was delegated.

3. **Provide clear instructions and define specific expectations:** Nothing is worse than being delegated a task, not being given instructions on how the task should be performed, not being told what is expected, and then working diligently to complete the task, only to be told it isn't what was wanted. If this has ever happened to you, you know how demoralizing and frustrating this situation is. Don't create this type of situation. Give specific instructions on what needs to be done and your expectation of the end result. This combination of proper instruction and setting expectations not only provides the correct delegation framework, but it also establishes criteria for how the work will be judged when the task is completed.

4. **Provide a safety net.** As a manager, when you are delegating tasks to your staff, particularly if it is a new experience for the employee, you must be willing to provide an appropriate level of support to help ensure the success of both the employee and the task.
   The type of support provided loosely falls into two categories: a safety net and mentoring. By a safety net, I mean creating an environment of help and protection by:

- Offering the needed resources and training.

- Allowing time to perform properly the delegated tasks.

- Helping employees navigate company politics.

- Providing instruction on how tasks should be performed.

As for mentoring, it will be discussed in Step #6.

5. **Let go and allow people to do their work.** If you delegate a task and then micro-manage it to the extent that you actually perform the task yourself, it's not delegation. That said, you should not totally divest yourself from the delegated task because, as the manager, you are still ultimately responsible for all work performed within your department. The trick is to walk that fine line between being overbearing and being non-participatory.

6. **Be mentoring and instructive.** Step #4 referred to creating an environment and culture of support. This step is related to providing direct instruction and advice to the person performing a specific, delegated task. I like to refer to this type of task-based instruction as a "learning moment," namely, just-in-time training on how to perform a specific task or how to deal with a specific situation.
   The level of instruction and/or advice provided should be based on a combination of the person's experience and the task's difficulty and political ramifications.

7. **Give credit to those doing the work.** As a manager, I have always believed in the philosophy of, "It's the team's success, or it's my failure." I ask you to consider making this your way of thinking also. By its nature, this philosophy causes you to raise the visibility of your staff's good work within the organization, which is motivating for your team and helps instill loyalty toward you. This approach also helps remind you that you are ultimately responsible for both your team's growth and your department's productivity and performance.

8. **Actively solicit feedback from your team.** Ask your team members whether they believe you have delegated tasks correctly, and whether

you, as their manager, have provided them with the best support possible to perform their tasks. The feedback you'll receive from these questions has the following advantages:

- It helps you grow as a leader by learning how you are perceived as a manager.

- It helps improve your team's performance by providing you with insights into better ways to delegate and support your staff.

- It shows your staff that you are willing to accept their suggestions, making you more approachable as a manager.

WHEN DELEGATING TO YOUR STAFF

When delegating to your staff, hierarchically, it's their job to follow your instructions, so you may ask, "Why is influence needed when delegating to your staff?" The answer is that getting them to do the task isn't enough—it's getting them to want to do the task and to do it well. Therefore, influence-based delegation primarily uses pull-type influence techniques, which attempt to motivate a person or group to want to perform the task at hand. These techniques include:

Influencer: Collaboration
Asking the person receiving the delegated task for their suggestions on the characteristics of the final deliverable and/or how a task should be completed gives them a greater feeling of ownership of the final product, increasing their motivation to do the task well.

Influencer: Vision
Painting a picture of a desired future vision that will result when the task being delegated has been completed allows the person assigned the task to understand its purpose and the required end state. This adds meaning to the task, thus increasing its importance in the eyes of the person performing it.

Influencer: Facts and logic

Describing a reason for the task using facts and logic with the goal of presenting a convincing argument as to why the task should be performed helps give it meaning and purpose.

Should you choose to use this approach to influence/motivate the person receiving the task, you should also provide your vision and business reason for the post-task, final state, and/or something more descriptive in nature. The reason is that facts and logic are generally not as persuasive as stories, emotional empathy, and business rationale.

Influencer: Emotional appeal

Using emotional stories, expressions, and words allows you to convey an emotional reason for performing the task. For this to work, of course, the delegated task itself must have an emotional element related to its completion.

Influencer: Delegating responsibility, not just the task

Allowing the individual to take ownership of the task gives the person a feeling of purpose and a greater feeling of accomplishment when the task is competed.

Influencer: Benefits over features

Describing why something should be done and the benefits it provides, rather than just explaining the mechanics of performing the task, gives greater meaning to the task and its accomplishment. This, in turn, provides a vision-based emotional platform for performing the task well and finishing it on time.

Influencer: Mutual gain

Framing the task to be performed in a manner that shows the benefit for those you are trying to motivate gives them a personal, not just a business, reason to produce high quality work and the desired outcome.

Influencer: Recognition and appreciation

Simply recognizing and appreciating people for their efforts, hard work, and positive results motivates them to do the same on the text task you assign them. Never underestimate the power of saying thank you.

WHEN DELEGATING TO YOUR PEERS

Properly delegating to your staff has many professional advantages. It helps you complete needed tasks. It helps your manager's team (you and your peers) work as a team for the greater good. Also, and potentially most important for your career, it places you in a leadership role among your peers because they are performing tasks based on your requests. This positions you for future promotions, and eventually, to be their manager, not just their peer.

When delegating to your peers, consider using the following influence techniques:

Influencer: Reciprocity

If you are willing to help your peers when they need assistance, they will be more likely to assist you when you need assistance.

Influencer: Taking the high road

When trying to influence a peer to assist you in a project, rather than making it all about you, talk about it from the company's, customer's, or another's perspective that will be of value, at least conceptually, for them also. It will be uncomfortable for them to say no to you if they feel your request is for the "greater good."

Influencer: Loyalty

If you are loyal to your peers when they need political, organizational, and/or budgetary assistance, they will be more likely to assist you when you need their help. Their help doesn't need to be in kind—it could simply be providing you with a needed contact, offering you a resource from their department, or doing something helpful personally.

Influencer: Liking

If your peers like you, it is easier to influence them to do something on your behalf. You don't have to be close friends or get together for lunch; you only need a comfortable business relationship and feelings of trust.

Influencer: Close relationship with your manager

One of the most reliable ways to gain influence over your peers is to be tightly aligned and close friends with your mutual boss. If your peers feel your manager is more likely to take your side than theirs, this gives you unstated delegated authority over others reporting to your manager.

Influencer: Cohen-Bradford currencies

As in all influence-based activities, try to gain an understanding of your peers' influence currencies. Subtly providing what they need can help you get what you need.

WHEN DELEGATING TO VENDORS

Regardless of the function a vendor performs or the products they provide, once the contract is signed, your vendor becomes part of your team. Unlike those working for your company, however, your goals are not their goals. They certainly want to help you, but to them, you're the client. Their goals are client engagement, profitability, follow-on contracts/orders, and their company's wellbeing. Never make the mistake of thinking your goals and your vendor's goals are the same—they're not. Therefore, you must influence them using different tactics, including those listed below:

Influencer: Offer to be a reference

Vendors are always looking for great new references to use in obtaining new clients. So, let them know that if things go well, you'll be happy to be a reference for them. They will work harder to ensure you're satisfied with their work and/or products.

Influencer: Refer other clients to them

In addition to offering to be a reference, take any opportunities that arise to use your contacts to refer new business to vendors. If vendors see you as a conduit for new business, they will go above and beyond to make sure you are happy.

Influencer: Pay them quickly

This technique works well on small vendors with cash flow issues. If you pay your bills quickly, sooner than industry norms, you will get a rapid response from your vendors because they know they will get paid quickly. For example, if your industry norm is payment in thirty days, pay vendors immediately upon receiving the invoice. If your company can handle the cash flow, this creates both goodwill and fast service. As they say, money talks.

Influencer: Work with two vendors, not one

If you have an ongoing contract for something like office supplies or consulting services, have two vendors, not one. This provides you greater influence over both vendors because of the competitive dynamic you create.

Influencer: Industry activism

If you are seen by the vendor as being well connected in your profession or industry, they will provide you with better service because of the two-edged sword that industry connections create. On the positive side for the vendor, you can provide them with contacts and act as an influential reference. On the negative side, if you dislike their service and casually tell your friends so at professional industry gatherings, it can hurt the vendor's reputation.

Influencer: Be a beta tester

If you have a contract with a vendor on a technical product, such as software or a piece of hardware, if given the opportunity to beta-test their product, agree to do so. Yes, it's a little additional work for you, but as a beta tester, you have the potential to speak to the product's developers and not just the customer service people. Then, if an issue arises in the future, long after the beta test has ended, if you are not getting the technical answers you need from the customer service people, you have the developers' contact info and can call them directly. One caution on using this technique—if you call the developers too often, they will stop answering your calls and refer you back to the technical support group. Only call the developers sparingly, in an emergency.

WHEN DELEGATING TO YOUR MANAGER

Delegating up is the art of using your manager to help you get things done. After all, completion of your tasks is their responsibility. Influence techniques you can use to manage up to your manager include:

Influencer: Producing quality work
Above all else, the best way to influence your manager and other superiors is to be seen as an important company resource with a reputation for producing high quality work. Whom would you be more likely to take advice from, a person known for generating great results or someone thought of as creating inferior quality products?

Influencer: Transparency
With transparency comes trust. When your manager believes you are honest and willing to tell the truth, good or bad, they are more likely to trust you. This trust will make your manager more likely to listen to your suggestions, perspective, and requests for assistance.

Influencer: Willingness to ask for help
Sometimes, the best way to get your manager's help is by simply asking. As said earlier, it may be part of your job requirement, but the completion of your tasks is still your manager's responsibility.

Influencer: Suggesting potential solutions
In addition to being willing to ask for help, whenever you ask your manager for help solving an issue, also provide a potential solution. In some cases, your manager will follow your suggestion. If not, it's still a win for you because it illustrates your ability and willingness to think on your own and not just ask for help.

Influence-Based Delegation Worksheet		
Delegation Influencers	**Person**	**Notes/Actions**
When delegating to your staff		
Collaboration		
Vision		
Facts and logic		
Emotional appeal		
Delegating responsibility, not just the task		
Benefits over features		
Mutual gain		
Recognition and appreciation		

Influence-Based Delegation Worksheet		
Delegation Influencers	Person	Notes/Actions
When delegating to your peers		
Reciprocity		
Taking the high road		
Loyalty		
Liking		
Close relationship with your manager		
Cohen-Bradford currencies		
When delegating to vendors		
Offer to be a reference		
Refer other clients to them		
Pay them quickly		
Work with two vendors, not one		
Industry activism		
Be a beta tester		

Influence-Based Delegation Worksheet

Delegation Influencers	Person	Notes/Actions
When delegating to your manager		
Producing quality work		
Transparency		
Willingness to ask for help		
Suggesting potential solutions		

INFLUENCE-BASED CONFLICT RESOLUTION

Nothing will suck the energy, creativity, productivity, and success out of an organization faster than internal conflict.

~Eric Bloom

In the workplace, two types of conflict affect our work:

1. Conflict between you and another person

2. Conflict between two other people, causing you a work issue

These two types of conflict are very different, even if the reason for the conflict is the same, because in #1, you're personally involved in the conflict, and in #2, you're observing a conflict between two different people. In the first case, you need to influence someone to end their conflict with you. In the second case, you must influence two other individuals to end their conflict with each other, at least long enough for you to get what you need from them.

CONFLICTS BETWEEN YOU AND ANOTHER PERSON

When the conflict is between you and another person, a number of standard conflict-resolution techniques can be used to improve the situation. They include: asking How, What, and Why questions; discussing the problem and not the person; and defining discussion ground rules (i.e., don't generalize, listen, don't just talk, avoid accusations, etc.). These conflict resolution techniques would be best learned attending a class or reading a book specifically on conflict. The goal of this chapter is to provide a few influence-based techniques to be used alone or in conjunction with more traditional conflict-resolution techniques. They are:

Influencer: Manage emotions using action/reaction
Your actions can cause the other person to act as you have, so execute the actions you want to see in the other person. For example:

- Ask questions showing your willingness to learn.

- Use friendly body language.

- Be calm and thoughtful.

- Focus on the present.

- Learn from the past, but don't dwell on it.

- Avoid accusations.

- Accept constructive feedback.

- Be respectful and accepting of different perspectives.

- Express your willingness to resolve the conflict.

Influencer: Mutual gain
When you frame the conflict's resolution as mutually beneficial, it has the dual benefits of, first, providing your advisory a reason to resolve the issue, and second, providing a structure for the two of you to work cooperatively to resolve the issue, making you part of the same team, with a common goal.

Potential tactical steps include:

1. Clearly define the issue causing the conflict.

2. Define your goals.

3. Define the other person's goals.

4. Define a future state that is advantageous to both of you.

5. Work together to develop a plan.

Influencer: Non-conflict related vision

Paint a picture that illustrates the advantages of working together on something other than your disagreement. For example, working on a project you have both been assigned and that will be a key contributor to next year's performance reviews.

Potential tactical steps include:

1. Agree to disagree on the issue causing the conflict.

2. Begin working on the new task together.

3. Hopefully, develop a trusting relationship that allows you also to solve the original conflict.

Influencer: Taking responsibility

If you proactively take ownership of your side of the conflict, then the other person may do the same, positioning both of you for the next steps toward resolution. This is a type of action/reaction influencer.

Potential tactical steps include:

1. Define your responsibility for the conflict.

2. Define a way to describe your role in the conflict that you feel comfortable with.

3. Meet the other person over coffee or tea at a private, neutral location, such as a conference room.

4. Say that you think you should take partial ownership for the conflict.

5. Ask the other person if they think they contributed to the conflict.

6. Suggest that you work together to solve the issue.

Note, if you truly feel the other person is totally to blame for the issue, do not use this technique; select a different approach.

Influencer: Finding a shared enemy

As the expression goes, "The enemy of my enemy is my friend." If you can find a common issue that both of you are working for or against, you can use this challenge to improve your working relationship.

CONFLICT BETWEEN TWO OTHER PEOPLE, CAUSING YOU A WORK ISSUE

How you resolve conflicts between two other people is dependent upon your relationship with the other people. In the workplace, these relationships generally fall into one of the following categories:

- Two people reporting to you

- One person reporting to you and another employee, vendor, or customer

- Your manager and a peer of your manager

- Two employees outside your department/organization

Two People Reporting to You

If the conflict is between two individuals who report to you, then you have a great deal of leverage in helping them resolve the issue. Because, as their manager, you have a high-level of organizational leverage over them both, consider using the following types of influence to help them work out the issue.

Influencer: Become the shared enemy
As said earlier in this chapter, "The enemy of my enemy is my friend." In this case, however, you conceptually become the enemy. Because you manage both of them, use a push-type influence.

Potential tactical steps include:

1. Let them know they will both be in trouble if they don't find a way to work together.

2. By you being the bad guy, you have given them an excuse to work together without either of them having to "give in."

3. As their manager, provide support as needed.

4. Work with them to resolve the issue.

Influencer: Provide mutual gain
This is the reverse of the previous strategy (becoming the shared enemy). In this case, rather than influence them through fear of loss, use the pull-type influence of anticipation of future gain.

Example tactic:

• Tell them that their annual performance reviews will be more favorable if they cooperate with each other and complete the project on time.

Influencer: Remove the issue
Sometimes the reason for conflict among your staff is you. This can happen when you give employees too much control over the process.

For example, a manager has two employees writing a request for proposal (RFP) for a new project. If they begin arguing over whether the contract should be fixed-price or time-and-materials, the manager can end the conflict by stepping in to make the decision for them.

One Person Reporting to You and Another Employee, Vendor, or Customer

When this situation occurs, you can advise your direct report on how to resolve the issue. If your staff member is responsible for the issue, then the discussion becomes a combination of corrective action and mentoring to correct their misstep.

If the issue was caused by a vendor, then you are still in control. If this is the case, you can use many of the same techniques described previously in the "two people reporting to you" scenario, because, conceptually, they both do, one as an employee and one as a hired, independent contractor.

Your Manager and a Peer of Your Manager

If the conflict is between your manager and your manager's peer, stay out of the way unless the conflict directly affects your work performance. In that case, work with your manager to ensure that the conflict doesn't ultimately affect your next performance review. This is done by managing up, potentially using the following influence techniques:

Influencer: Asking leading questions

Ask your manager a leading question with the intent of letting them come to the conclusion that the conflict between the two departments should not affect your job performance.

Examples of leading questions include:

- Can you think of a way the conflict with the other department will not hurt my next performance review?

- Do you think the conflict we're having with the other department is hurting our department's overall productivity?

- Given the conflict we are having with the other department, what can we do to stop this from hurting my next performance review?

Influencer: Direct request

Sometimes the best way to get your manager's support is simply to ask. In this case, ask your manager not to allow the issue with another department to influence your next performance review.

Examples of leading questions include:

- Given the conflict we're having with the other department, could you please make sure this doesn't affect my next performance review?

Two Employees Outside of Your Department/Organization

In this scenario, once again, you have no direct control over those involved in the dispute. Your influence in this situation will hinge on your organizational level, and the potential you have for giving them pleasure or inflicting pain if they can't set aside their issues long enough for you to get you what you need. These two-sided influencers are listed below.

Influencer: Become the shared enemy

You are the shared enemy who will cause them to rally as team. If you hold an influential position within your company, they may be more intimidated and concerned about staying on your good side than they are angry about their existing conflict. Ideally, working together to meet your project needs will provide the conduit for long-term agreement. If not, at least you were able to get your request fulfilled.

Influencer: Provide mutual gain

Like earlier in the chapter, this is the reverse of the previous strategy (become the shared enemy). In this case, use the pull-type influence of creating anticipation of future gain. It is mutually beneficial to manage those you are trying to influence to get along and get your work done. Subtly offer to send their manager an email describing the great work accomplished on your behalf. This not only motivates them based upon anticipation of your kind words, but it also leaves the lingering, unspoken threat of sending a negative email to their manager if you are displeased with their service.

Influence-Based Conflict Worksheet

Conflict: _____

Conflict Influencers	Notes/Actions
Conflicts between you and another person	
Manage emotions using action/reaction	
Mutual gain	
Non-conflict related vision	
Taking responsibility	
Finding a shared enemy	
Two people reporting to you	
Become the shared enemy	
Provide mutual gain	
Remove the issue	
Your manager and a peer of your manager	
Asking leading questions	
Direct request	
Two employees outside your department/organization	
Become the shared enemy	
Provide mutual gain	

INFLUENCE-BASED PRESENTATION SUCCESS

I've learned that people will forget what you said, people will forget what you did, but people will never forget how you made them feel.

~Maya Angelou

This chapter describes how to achieve your business goals through successful presentation using influence techniques before, during, and after meetings to gain agreement.

At a high-level, this four-step process concentrates on your presentation's audience, rather than on the presentation itself. This process' objective is to gain agreement and approval of your proposal before the meeting begins, gain official approval during the meeting, and then move the agreement toward implementation through post-presentation communication with the key decision makers.

STEP 1: PARTICIPANT RESEARCH

The first step in this process is researching the participants who will be in the room or connected virtually during your presentation. This step's objective is to learn as much as you can about your audience so you can:

- Properly prepare your presentation.

- Decide who needs to be influenced and what types of influence are required prior to your meeting.

- Avoid being surprised by anything when your presentation begins.

- Portray yourself in the best possible light to enhance your professional reputation.

To the extent possible, it's ideal to know the following about each meeting participant:

- What is their organizational level?

- What is their knowledge of the topic?

- What is their professional discipline?

- Are they friend or foe?

- Will they benefit or be hurt by your proposal?

- Were they forced to attend and/or do they care about your topic?

- Will they try to forward their agenda, regardless of your content?

- Do you have past successes and challenges with the participants?

You should also understand the relationship between the participants, including:

- What is the reporting structure between the various participants?

- What are the interpersonal dynamics between those in the room?

- Who are the key decision makers?

Understand what the participants want, for example:

- To make a decision (about you, your project, your product, etc.)

- To learn something of interest

- To prepare for action (new skills, insights, information, etc.)

- To receive a status update

- To help you succeed

- To stop you from succeeding

- To elevate themselves

Compare yourself to those in the meeting based on:

- Relative knowledge of the topic.

- Relative professional stature/level.

Finally, understand the presentation's situational dynamics in regard to:

- The quality of your presentation.

- Your preparation.

- Comparison of you to other speakers/proposals.

- Importance of the topic to you.

- Importance of the topic to your audience.

STEP 2: PRE-MEETING INFLUENCE TACTICS

With your Step 1 research completed, you're positioned to define and implement your pre-meeting influence tactics. The objective of these tactics is to guarantee your presentation's success by quietly getting approval from all the decision makers prior to the meeting in the following way:

1. Starting with the decision makers, speak with each of the meeting participants one-on-one, in person or by phone, to assess their willingness to support your proposal.

   a. If they agree to approve your proposal, thank them and ask if they have any suggestions for improvement.

   b. If they do not agree to approve your proposal (or have reservations), ask specifically, "What needs to change to gain your approval?"

2. Make small changes to your proposal and/or presentation based on the advice you receive from all your conversations.

3. Email each of the participants:

   a. For those who agreed to approve your proposal, thank them for their time, support, and suggestions. Then tell them how you changed your proposal based on their great advice.

   b. For those who did not agree with you, thank them for their time and thoughtful suggestions. Then tell them how you changed your proposal based on their insight and feedback. Then ask them again if they would support you based on the changes. Repeat this step, if needed. If you realize they will never support you, spend your time on other participants who show more promise.

The above steps provide the following advantages:

- You know where each person stands regarding your proposal.

- Your one-on-one attention may have moved people who were undecided to your side.

- By making small changes to your proposal/presentation based on others' advice, they will have a small feeling of ownership in your proposal, helping to influence them to agree with you when the time comes.

- These small changes also show that you listened and acted on what they told you, evoking feelings of reciprocity and liking.

STEP 3: MEETING INFLUENCE TACTICS

Finally, it's meeting time. It is imperative that you control the room because you have spent all this time preparing your presentation and gaining buy-in from the participants. The danger is, if your presentation gets off track or you are asked questions you did not anticipate and cannot answer, your proposal may be rejected or the decision postponed until these additional questions can be answered.

Influence techniques you can use during your presentation to keep on track and help ensure a positive outcome are:

Influencer: Stand in the position of power

When giving a presentation, where you physically stand can make a big difference. It's a type of spatial presence. The way to use it to your advantage is to stand in the same physical spot an important person has just vacated. If you do this, some of their authority will be subconsciously passed to you.

Example tactic:

- If you are introduced at a company meeting by the CEO who is standing three feet to the left of the lectern, you should stand in exactly the same spot.

- If there are many speakers presenting proposals to senior management, stand in the same spot as a person whose project was approved.

- Conversely, if the person who spoke before you had their project rejected, physically stand in a different location when you present your project.

Influencer: Smile and use eye contact

By smiling and using eye contact, you are increasing your likability and perceived honesty. Also, because you're smiling, it's likely you can get the audience to smile. It's called mirroring, which is why when someone yawns, other people often yawn. If your audience smiles, body language research has shown that it will improve their mood.

Influencer: Show confidence and strength

When you are the presenter, you are the alpha dog in the room, regardless of who is sitting in the audience. You are standing; they are sitting. You know the material being presented; they are waiting to hear your thoughts. Subtly use this to your advantage. If you look, feel, and sound confident in what you are saying, people are more likely to believe you. One caution—there is a big difference between being confident and being boastful. Confidence brings respect and influence; boasting brings dislike and disdain.

Influencer: Recognition and gratitude

Never underestimate the value of saying thank you. At the beginning of the meeting, if you publicly thank the people who gave you advice on your proposal (see Step 2), you are invoking various types of influence, including:

- Gratitude, which is a Cohen-Bradford currency.

- Delegated authority, indirectly, from those who had input into the proposal.

- Liking, one of Cialdini's Six Principles of Persuasion.

- Action/reaction—you spoke nicely about them; they may speak nicely about you.

Influencer: Participant involvement

With involvement comes understanding and ownership. If you can get the participants into a lively and positive discussion about your proposal, then you are more likely to get agreement. Also, if they state any concerns, you can immediately address their concerns with the goal of putting their minds at ease.

Influencer: Seeded questions

"Seeded questions" are questions you have requested someone else in the meeting to ask as a way to get the conversation flowing and/or to raise a point you would like to discuss. This is a great way to introduce topics that, for some reason, you didn't want to formally include in your proposal.

STEP 4: POST-MEETING INFLUENCE TACTICS

Now that you have won the battle (your proposal was approved), make sure you win the peace (are able to move your proposal forward). One of the best ways to start your initiative on the right foot and cement ongoing support is to thank the people in the meeting who approved your proposal. A short, individually written thank you email shows your gratitude for their assistance and positions you for future requests as needed.

Influence-Based Presentation Success
Step 1 and 2: Participant Research Checklist

Information on each individual meeting participant:

- ☐ Organizational level?
- ☐ Knowledge of the topic?
- ☐ Professional discipline?
- ☐ Friend or foe?
- ☐ Will benefit or be hurt by your proposal?
- ☐ Forced to be there and/or don't care?
- ☐ Will try to forward their agenda?
- ☐ Past successes and challenges?

Relationship between the participants:

- ☐ Reporting structures?
- ☐ Interpersonal dynamics?
- ☐ Key decision makers?

What participants want:

- ☐ To make a decision?
- ☐ To learn something of interest?
- ☐ To prepare for action?
- ☐ To receive a status update?
- ☐ To help you succeed?
- ☐ To stop you from succeeding?
- ☐ To ensure personal gain?

Compare yourself to those in the meeting:

- ☐ Relative knowledge of the topic?
- ☐ Relative professional stature/level?

Situational dynamics in regard to:

- ☐ Quality of your presentation?
- ☐ Amount of presentation preparation?
- ☐ Comparison of you to other speakers/proposals?

☐   Importance of the topic to you?

☐   Importance of the topic to your audience?

If the presentation is for approval of an important proposal:

1.   Speak with each decision maker one-on-one to assess their willingness to support your proposal.

2.   Make small changes to your presentation/proposal based on their feedback.

3.   Tell them (via email, phone, or in-person) about the changes you made based on their insight and feedback to give them a feeling of ownership and support for your proposal.

Influence-Based Presentation Success Worksheet
Step 3: Meeting Influence Tactics

Presentation Name: _____

On Stage Influencers	Action Plan
Stand in a position of power	
Smile and use eye contact	
Show confidence and strength	
Recognition and gratitude	
Participant involvement	
Seeded questions	

INFLUENCE-BASED PROJECT MANAGEMENT

Influence is to project management as lead foil and solder are to stained glass windows; they both provide the bond that allows beautiful things to be created.

~Eric Bloom

While the use of innovative influence techniques is of great value in all job roles, it's crucially important for project managers (PMs). PMs are usually in the unenviable position of being responsible for completing a task without the benefit of authority over the people who are doing the work or the budget needed to acquire needed resources. These necessary assets are controlled by others, and it is the PM's role to convince those controlling the needed assets to allocate them to the project. Without the assets, the project fails, and the PM is blamed.

I generally divide stakeholders into two categories: those who can cause you pleasure or pain during the change, and those who cause pleasure or pain once the change is implemented. These two distinct stakeholder types must be influenced in different ways because you are asking them for different things. During the project, you ask your stakeholders for resources and approvals. During the implementation, you ask people and/or organizational cultures to change, which is discussed in Chapter 22: Influence-Based Organizational Change.

For a project to succeed, various groups of people must support it. If one of these groups falls short, then the entire project is at risk. These groups are:

- Project stakeholders who provide people

- Project stakeholders who provide budgets and other resources

- Dotted-line employees working on the project but reporting to other managers

- Compliance and regulatory staff that must approve the project

PROJECT STAKEHOLDERS WHO PROVIDE PEOPLE

Dotted-line resources are those who do not administratively report to the person directing their day-to-day work activities. For example, a project manager working with a software developer on loan from the company's IT department.

If dotted-line resources don't work directly for you, you must influence them and their administrative manager.

The techniques for influencing and motivating your dotted-line employees are much the same as those used to influence your staff. Influencing the managers of your dotted-line resources requires different techniques, because the goal is different. Your goal for them is to get continued support for your projects. To do so, consider using the following influence techniques:

Influencer: Treating resources well
When administrative managers provide resources to other groups, they expect their people to be treated with respect, integrity, and fairness. If you treat your dotted-line resources well, not only will they want to work for you again, but the administrative manager will also be influenced to continue to provide resources for your projects.

Influencer: Following administrative manager's processes
Even though an employee is on loan to your department, their administrative manager is still responsible for their performance reviews, training, career pathway, and other related manager/employee activities. Do all you can to assist the administrative manager with manage-

rial tasks. Provide job performance input and fulfill any other requests from the administrative manager that make it easier for them to do their job. This cooperation evokes reciprocity, liking, cooperation, and other positive feelings that will make it more likely for the administrative manager to prioritize your needs over those of someone who makes their job more difficult.

PROJECT STAKEHOLDERS WHO PROVIDE BUDGETS AND OTHER RESOURCES

In addition to people, projects often need other resources, like access to corporate data, computer equipment, trucks, cash, and other non-human assets.

You must influence these stakeholders in two ways. First, gain their agreement that your project is worthwhile. Second, get them to prioritize your project over other potential recipients of resources. To accomplish this, consider using the following influence techniques:

Influencer: Reciprocity
When people loan you resources, providing them some type of ongoing value in return helps ensure your continued use of these resources. This is the case because they feel reciprocal obligation. Their fear is that if they no longer provide you with the resources you need, you will withdraw the ongoing value you are giving to them.
As a simple example, if you provide their department needed client data, this unstated reciprocal agreement can continue as long as this data is of greater value to them than the cost of loaning you their resources.

Influencer: Liking
If the administrative manager likes you more than the others they are supporting by lending resources, you are more likely to receive a higher priority when resources become scarce.

Influencer: Cohen-Bradford currencies
Try to gain an understanding of the administrative manager's desired

influence currencies, and, to the extent possible, use them in a way that helps ensure you get the resources you need to be successful in your projects and initiatives.

DOTTED-LINE EMPLOYEES

As previously mentioned, dotted-line resources are people who do not administratively report to the person directing their day-do-day work activities, in this case, you as the PM. Influencing dotted-line employees to work hard on your projects is based on two primary factors: first, motivating employees to produce high quality work; and second, maintaining continued support from their administrative managers, which was previously discussed in the section, "Project Stakeholders Who Provide People."

Motivating your dotted-line resources is virtually the same as discussed in Chapter 23: Influence-Based Delegating. If your dotted-line resource is working on multiple projects simultaneously, you must continuously influence them to prioritize your tasks over others. You can accomplish this by making sure your project is a priority for the administrative manager and that you continually communicate with them regarding your project's importance to the company and/or their career.

COMPLIANCE AND REGULATORY STAFF

If you work in a regulated industry, such as financial services or healthcare, there are specialized corporate departments that keep track of these industry regulations and make certain the company follows them. If your project falls under the compliance department's jurisdiction, involve them early, involve them often, and follow their direction. If you don't, your project could be canceled, you could lose your job, or you could go to jail, depending on the regulatory rules/laws you failed to follow.

In this case, the goal is not to influence them to change their mind regarding regulatory matters, but to secure their time in reviewing and approving your project's compliance plan. Because you are in a regulated environment, you may need their ongoing approval to move forward on your project. In other words, you don't want to miss project deadlines simply because you could not get interim or final approvals from the compliance department because you couldn't get their attention.

Influence techniques that can be used to gain the compliance department's attention include:

Influencer: Communication

We've all heard the expression, "It's easier to say 'I'm sorry' than 'May I?'" Not in this case. It is important to be proactive and contact them before they come looking for you. They will appreciate your cooperation and be easier to work with if you exhibit a willingness to comply with their instructions.

Influencer: Liking

You are more likely to receive needed attention for moving your project forward if they like you.

Influencer: Provide deliverables early

When the compliance department asks you for project plans, documents, or other items to review, provide them as soon as possible. If you respect their sense of urgency, they will feel more obligated to respond to your issues on a timely basis.

Influencer: Accept constructive feedback

When the compliance department gives you advice, show a willingness to take it to heart and act upon it immediately. If the need arises to provide them feedback, such as pointing out that approval of your documents is too slow, they are more likely to listen to you because you listened to them.

Influence-Based Project Management Worksheet

Influencers	Person	Notes/Actions
Project stakeholders providing people		
Treating resources well		
Following administrative manager's processes		
Project stakeholders provide budgets and other resources		
Reciprocity		
Liking		
Cohen-Bradford currencies		
Compliance and regulatory staff		
Communication		
Liking		
Provide deliverables early		
Accept constructive feedback		

INFLUENCE-BASED LEADERSHIP

*Leadership is not about titles, positions or flowcharts.
It is about one life influencing another.*

~John C. Maxwell

In many ways, this chapter is a review of all the concepts discussed throughout the book because leadership itself is such a broad and multi-faceted topic.

Whether you work in the mailroom or boardroom, the ability to influence others is a key component of leadership success. C-suite members must work on an equal footing with other C-suite level executives, project managers must motivate and direct their dotted-line resources, and individual contributors must often lead others toward a task's completion.

Leadership comes naturally to some people and must be meticulously learned by others. In either case, your leadership skills can be greatly enhanced through the ongoing study of leadership techniques and best practices. This chapter discusses various influence-based concepts, techniques, and tactics designed to enhance your leadership proficiency and effectiveness.

These influencers are:

Influence topic: Importance of personal connection
As a leader, get to know and understand the people on your team. All interpersonal communication, including negotiation, change management, conflict resolution, difficult conversations, motivation, approval requests, delegation, and others, are improved if you have

previously established a trusting personal connection with the other person.

Influence topic: Explaining the influence of ROI
Understanding the ROI of learning and using influence-based techniques has two primary advantages. First, it motivates you personally to enhance your existing leadership style with influence-based techniques. Second, if you teach these techniques to your staff, they too can be more effective and efficient in the work you have asked them to perform.

Influence topic: Navigating barriers to influence
Learning to recognize influence barriers makes it easier for you either to navigate around them or address the issues and work through them.

Influence topic: Understanding the seven key influence strategies
Different situations require different influence strategies and tactics. Understanding these different strategies encourages you to thoughtfully decide which strategies and techniques to use, rather than simply using your favorite techniques in all situations.

Influence topic: Push-based influence
Sometimes, the most appropriate way to influence others is simply to tell them to do something, rather than trying to motivate them to do it on their own. Just telling people what to do takes less time, but it can be demotivating to the employee and, ultimately, lower job satisfaction and team morale.

Influence topic: Pull-based influence
Pull influences, like collaboration, vision, and the use of facts and logic to motivate people to act on their own, rather than being pushed to act, enhances employee job satisfaction, reduces attrition, increases employee morale, enhances your reputation as a leader, and creates a higher level of quality.

Influence topic: Using influential communication
The use of influential communication, such as storytelling, asking purposeful questions, using problem/vision statements, and selecting the best physical location and time for discussions can greatly help you gain acceptance of your leadership vision.

Influence topic: Using Cialdini's Six Principles of Persuasion
Understanding and tactically using Cialdini's Six Principles of Persuasion can greatly enhance your ability to get things done.

Influence topic: Understanding Cohen-Bradford influence currencies
Understanding the various types of Cohen-Bradford influence currencies can help you decide which techniques will work on whom, thus enabling you to maximize your influence-based activities by tailoring them on an individual basis.

Influence topic: Using action/reaction influencers
This subtle type of influence allows you to gently influence others' actions simply by the way you act toward them.

Influence topic: Building your influential professional brand
The stronger your professional brand, the greater your influence. This is because people are more willing to take advice, suggestions, and direction from those they respect and admire.

Influence topic: Understanding your Influence Power Rating (IPR)
Understanding your IPR allows you to strategically enhance your core influence characteristics and tactically assess your current situational influence to maximize your short-term and long-term success.

PRACTICE MAKES PERFECT

Good, better, best. Never let it rest.
Until your good is better and your better is best.

~St. Jerome (and my mom)

Part 1 of this book discussed a variety of important, influence-related concepts, definitions, techniques, tactics, and tips. In Part 2, the IPR calculation brought together two key influence-related concepts. The first concept helps you identify and build your ability to impress, interact with, and gain the respect of others. The second concept is designed to provide an understanding of your ability to influence a particular person or group on a specific topic at a specific moment. Part 3 provides specific instruction on how the various influence concepts, techniques, tips, and tricks discussed in Parts 1 and 2 can be used to enhance your success in workplace-related, interpersonal activities.

All the knowledge you gained reading this book will be for naught if you do not practice and internalize what you have learned. Realistically, you can't use all the techniques described in this book—there are too many. I have what I like to call my seventy-two-hour rule. This rule states that if don't try at least one of the techniques learned within seventy-two hours, then, most likely, you will never use them. Maximize your ROI in reading this book by following these steps:

1. Think of the technique that most resonated with you.

2. Make a list of potential work and personal scenarios where this technique can be used with low risk, for example, while watching a football game with friends.

3. Practice this one technique again and again in different scenarios

until you have internalized when to use it, who to use it on, and how to measure if it's working.

4. Once you have internalized the technique and truly made it your own, begin to use it in other, appropriate situations.

5. Go back to Step 1 and select another technique.

If you follow these five, repeating steps, over time you will dramatically enhance your ability not only to influence others as opportunities present themselves, but you will also be able to use your newfound and heavily-practiced influence repertoire strategically as a way to enhance your success in negotiation, delegation, conflict resolution, and all other aspects of interpersonal communication.

Good luck!

ABOUT THE AUTHOR

Eric Bloom is the Executive Director of the IT Management and Leadership Institute. He is also a TEDx speaker, a #1 Amazon bestselling author, a former nationally syndicated columnist, a contributing writer to CIO.com, a technologist, and a research advisor for International Data Corporation (IDC). Prior to his current role, Eric was a senior IT executive at various firms such as Fidelity Investments, Monster.com, and Independence Investments.

As a recognized thought leader, Eric speaks, instructs, and writes on interpersonal communication influence, negotiation, organizational change, and other related employee interactions.

Eric is also the past president of the National Speakers Association of New England, a Certified Professional Speaker (CSP), and the author of various books, including:

- *Productivity Driven Success: Hidden Secrets of Organizational Efficiency* (#1 Amazon bestseller)

- The CIO's Guide to Staff Needs, Growth, and Productivity

- Your IT Career: Get Noticed, Get Promoted, and Build Your Professional Brand

- Manager Mechanics: Tips and Advice for First-Time Managers

Eric holds undergraduate degrees in Computer Systems and Accounting from Bentley University and an MBA from Babson College.

Contact Eric at eric@ITMLInstitute.org, follow him on Twitter at @EricPBloom, or visit www.ITMLInstitute.org and www.OfficeInfluence.com.

44038875R00158

Made in the USA
Middletown, DE
04 May 2019